KV-372-078

WITHDRAWN
FROM THE LIBRARY OF
UNIVERSITY OF ULSTER

Corporate Governance:
A Survey
of OECD Countries

UNIVERSITY OF ULSTER LIBRARY

OECD

ORGANISATION FOR ECONOMIC CO-OPERATION AND DEVELOPMENT

100476081

ORGANISATION FOR ECONOMIC CO-OPERATION AND DEVELOPMENT

Pursuant to Article 1 of the Convention signed in Paris on 14th December 1960, and which came into force on 30th September 1961, the Organisation for Economic Co-operation and Development (OECD) shall promote policies designed:

- to achieve the highest sustainable economic growth and employment and a rising standard of living in member countries, while maintaining financial stability, and thus to contribute to the development of the world economy;
- to contribute to sound economic expansion in member as well as non-member countries in the process of economic development; and
- to contribute to the expansion of world trade on a multilateral, non-discriminatory basis in accordance with international obligations.

The original member countries of the OECD are Austria, Belgium, Canada, Denmark, France, Germany, Greece, Iceland, Ireland, Italy, Luxembourg, the Netherlands, Norway, Portugal, Spain, Sweden, Switzerland, Turkey, the United Kingdom and the United States. The following countries became members subsequently through accession at the dates indicated hereafter: Japan (28th April 1964), Finland (28th January 1969), Australia (7th June 1971), New Zealand (29th May 1973), Mexico (18th May 1994), the Czech Republic (21st December 1995), Hungary (7th May 1996), Poland (22nd November 1996), Korea (12th December 1996) and the Slovak Republic (14th December 2000). The Commission of the European Communities takes part in the work of the OECD (Article 13 of the OECD Convention).

Publié en français sous le titre :
Gouvernement d'entreprise : panorama des pays de l'OCDE

© OECD 2004

Permission to reproduce a portion of this work for non-commercial purposes or classroom use should be obtained through the Centre français d'exploitation du droit de copie (CFC), 20, rue des Grands-Augustins, 75006 Paris, France, tel. (33-1) 44 07 47 70, fax (33-1) 46 34 67 19, for every country except the United States. In the United States permission should be obtained through the Copyright Clearance Center, Customer Service, (508)750-8400, 222 Rosewood Drive, Danvers, MA 01923 USA, or CCC Online: *www.copyright.com*. All other applications for permission to reproduce or translate all or part of this book should be made to OECD Publications, 2, rue André-Pascal, 75775 Paris Cedex 16, France.

Foreword

The dramatic collapse of major companies over the past few years has focused the minds of governments, regulators, companies, investors and the general public on the weaknesses in corporate governance systems and the associated threat posed to the integrity of financial markets. The response is ongoing and encompasses numerous elements, including new institutions, for example, to oversee the accounting and audit profession, new laws to strengthen internal controls and new standards or soft law such as principles of corporate governance and codes of ethics. This response phase is likely to continue for some time, and some countries will be slower in implementing changes. However, the balance of the debate will begin to turn to whether the new measures have indeed succeeded in correcting the systemic weaknesses that have been identified and whether there are new issues requiring action of some sort.

Throughout this period of response to new challenges, the OECD Principles of Corporate Governance have provided specific guidance which is reflected in legislative and regulatory initiatives or in national principles and codes in all of OECD's 30 member countries and in a number of other countries as well. The Financial Stability Forum has named them as one of the Twelve Key Standards for Sound Financial Systems. The OECD Principles underpin the corporate governance component of the World Bank/IMF Reports on Observance of Standards and Codes (ROSC). To ensure that the Principles continue to meet evolving challenges, in 2002 OECD Ministers called for a survey of developments and assessment of the Principles to be completed by 2004. This review is being undertaken by the OECD Steering Group on Corporate Governance as a priority of the Organisation.

This report, Corporate Governance: A Survey of OECD Countries, is part of the review and assessment of the Principles. It examines the need for reform in the OECD area and records how individual countries have responded to the challenges up until now. It also identifies emerging issues, including those requiring further elaboration in the Principles. A second report, which has been issued separately, focuses on experience in economies outside the OECD where the OECD, in co-operation with the World Bank Group and other sponsors, has been conducting Regional Corporate Governance Roundtables – in Asia, Latin America, Russia, Eurasia and South East Europe – identifying regional priorities for improving the corporate governance framework. The review of the Principles has also entailed extensive consultations with, inter alia, business, investors and civil society organisations from both member and non-member countries. In January 2004, the OECD also invited comments from the public on a draft revision of the Principles.

Three themes are examined in this report:

- First, the report documents the forces that have contributed to short-term corporate crises as well as those that are likely to lead to lower corporate valuations, inefficient allocation of capital, higher cost of finance, and lower growth – issues that are important from a long-term perspective. The report highlights the role played by weaknesses in the corporate governance framework in cases of crises, and how the Principles anticipated many of the problems which have now become apparent. It suggests that more attention to implementing the Principles, including independent judgement by both boards and auditors, would have helped limit the losses associated with the steep decline of equity prices after 2000. The report also summarises the growing body of empirical work showing the importance of corporate governance in determining company performance and economic growth.

- Second, the report reviews the range of OECD experiences and examines how the Principles can bring underlying problems into focus and how they point the direction for action by both the authorities and the corporate sector.

- Third, the report examines how different member countries are dealing with their corporate governance problems in order to achieve the aims outlined in the OECD Principles. The needs identified in different countries include strengthening board oversight of management, improving the potential for the exercise of informed ownership by shareholders, and increasing attention to conflicts of interest. Learning from the experience of other countries as each one tackles similar issues is a key aspect of OECD work in all policy areas, and will need to be further developed in the corporate governance field as new legislative, regulatory and private measures unfold.

This report underlines the importance of principles that set out clear objectives when dealing with the corporate governance framework. There is just too much variation between countries and even between companies and sectors for detailed prescriptions to be helpful. Nevertheless, such principles leave open the question of how policies and institutions can be most effectively adapted to deal with a situation of inadequate corporate governance. Answers to that question can be found through regular policy dialogue which is one of the hallmarks of OECD work.

While the OECD Council at Ministerial level is expected to consider revised Principles that build upon this assessment when it meets again in May 2004, it is already clear that improving corporate governance arrangements requires sustained efforts for the foreseeable future.

Donald J. Johnston
Secretary-General

CORPORATE GOVERNANCE: A SURVEY OF OECD COUNTRIES – ISBN 92-64-10605-7 – © OECD 2004

Acknowledgements. *This report was prepared by Grant Kirkpatrick of the OECD Corporate Affairs Division and is being released following review and declassification by the OECD Steering Group on Corporate Governance. Special thanks go to Mats Isaksson, Laura Holliday and colleagues in the Corporate Affairs Division.*

Table of Contents

Tables

CORPORATE GOVERNANCE: A SURVEY OF OECD COUNTRIES – ISBN 92-64-10605-7 – © OECD 2004

ISBN 92-64-10605-7
Survey of Corporate Governance Developments in OECD Countries
© OECD 2004

Executive Summary

The Survey forms part of the assessment of the *OECD Principles of Corporate Governance* requested by Ministers in 2002. A report covering the experience of the Regional Corporate Governance Roundtables in using the Principles as a common framework for discussions leading to Regional Corporate Governance White Papers has also been prepared. In short, the Survey confirms the relevance of the Principles for considering what needs to be done on the part of both the authorities and companies to improve corporate governance. However, the report also reveals that translating the Principles into specific action is often challenging and several new policy issues have also emerged making it important to review the Principles in the light of recent experience.

Policy concern with corporate governance issues has been driven in recent years primarily by a series of corporate scandals and failures in a number of countries. Although bankruptcies are to some extent a cyclical phenomenon, and especially so following an asset price bubble, systemic weaknesses have also been evident. This was particularly true with respect to financial disclosure and audit integrity but at a deeper level such weaknesses do raise serious questions about whether boards have been able to exercise independent judgement with respect to the oversight of management. The importance of preventing such weaknesses is already a key element of the Principles which were widely accepted in member countries. This raises the question as to why the weaknesses were not foreseen and how implementation might have been better organised.

Policy interest in corporate governance needs to be seen in a forward looking manner and not just as an enforcement exercise to deal with past misdeeds. Changing financial markets, including the relative decline in banking and the rapid rise of institutional investors, and the growth of savings for pensions in most member countries, have implications for the corporate governance framework as does changing business circumstances. While corporate governance arrangements can be expected to adjust spontaneously there is often a need for policy to facilitate adjustments.

Member countries are also concerned to stimulate growth and employment in an increasingly competitive environment. There is now a growing body of empirical research linking certain key aspects of corporate governance arrangements both to firm performance and to growth. Nevertheless, so long as key functional aspects are met, there does not appear to be a unique institutional or legal structure for ensuring growth.

10

In response to both short term pressures and longer term considerations, member countries have been active in taking policy initiatives. First, a number have been involved in reviewing their company law and in even more countries legal changes have tightened audit functions, increased transparency and improved the role of shareholders. Second, nearly all member countries have now introduced national principles for governance based in great measure on the Principles. The balance between legal changes, regulation and self-regulation/ voluntary arrangements has varied quite widely. Taken as a whole, it is clear that attention has shifted toward implementation and enforcement of measures to meet the main features advocated by the Principles.

Many national principles are of very recent origin so that conclusions must remain tentative. Nevertheless, it appears that national principles have tended to focus on the operation of the board and on transparency with much less attention given to the role of shareholders. Where the latter is covered, compliance has been relatively limited. There appears to be a tendency to move from strictly voluntary principles to "comply or explain" as an implementation principle, although monitoring of compliance is in general under-developed. Finally, in a number of cases there has been a tendency for principles to enumerate "best practice" in some detail with the danger that they might become increasingly prescriptive.

One of the most fundamental questions concerns the rights of shareholders. It has become clear in many countries that the actual role of shareholders in the election of board members, the approval of major corporate decisions and demanding accountability by the board is in practice quite limited. Attention is now turning in some countries towards making it both easier to vote, also cross-border, and for it to be more meaningful, as for example by facilitating votes on remuneration questions. A key question is the role of institutional investors: should they use their voting rights and if so, under what conditions? In a number of countries institutions are being urged to make their voting policy transparent. The protection of minority shareholders is another important issue with consideration being given in some countries to *ex ante* enforcement measures such as cumulative voting and the possibility to nominate "minority directors".

Nearly all countries accept that stakeholders have a role in corporate governance and have legal rights which need to be enforced. Nevertheless, creditor rights may be difficult to enforce and bankruptcy processes lengthy and inefficient. With respect to employees, performance enhancing mechanisms are now more widespread and seem to have a positive effect. Securing pension claims of past and present employees has emerged as an important issue in a number of countries where private pension provision is predominant. One area where the legal rights of stakeholders needs improvement is in the area of "whistle-blower" protection which is also important in implementing anti-bribery measures.

As part of the policy reaction to fears about financial market integrity, there have been numerous initiatives by the authorities to improve disclosure and transparency. The whole process has been placed under examination, from internal preparation of financial reports and internal controls through to the role of the board in approving the disclosure, the accounting standards being used and the integrity of the external audit process. The responsibility of boards and their audit committees (or similar bodies) have been tightened and a number of countries have now introduced public oversight of the setting of accounting and audit standards. This process places professional self-monitoring under tighter oversight. Moreover, in an increasing number of countries auditors are being restricted in the non-audit services that they can perform in order to reduce incentives that might lead to diminished independence in the implementation of audit standards. Some form of auditor rotation is also being introduced. Providers of financial information such as analysts and rating agencies also face potential conflicts of interest that are leading to both structural remedies and to greater disclosure, the balance varying across countries. Non-financial disclosure, including the provision of information useful to stakeholders such as human resource policies, is also coming in for greater attention from both some governments and civil society organisations.

The authorities have given priority to improving the operation of boards, which it is widely considered have not adequately performed their oversight role. The most dominant theme has been to increase the number of "independent" board members and in several countries there has also been concern to improve their quality by both training and by the use of more systematic recruitment. Independence is, however, not always clearly defined and may not result in boards "capable of independent judgement" unless accompanied by other changes such as to the nomination and election system. Board members independent of management are regarded as important for roles where the board might have a conflict of interest such as in the determination of executive and members remuneration, nomination and audit. But in a number of member countries, independence from a major shareholder is an equally important issue. Remuneration questions including termination payments have become a key issue in a number of countries prompting the question as to whether national principles and independent board members are enough to control the problem, or whether the authorities need to go further by giving greater power to shareholders, and finally through more stringent regulation.

The ethical environment of the company has taken on new importance as attention has shifted to how the Principles can be implemented. Observing ethical standards such as those embodied in the OECD *Guideline for Multinational Enterprises* and the *Anti-Bribery Convention*, is widely regarded as an important function of the board as is ensuring compliance with existing regulatory and legal requirements. In a number of countries, companies are also encouraged to create their own codes of conduct.

CORPORATE GOVERNANCE: A SURVEY OF OECD COUNTRIES – ISBN 92-64-10605-7 – © OECD 2004

Introduction

In the aftermath of the Asian financial crisis in 1997, the OECD Council Meeting at Ministerial level called upon the OECD to develop, in conjunction with national governments, other relevant international organisations and the private sector, a set of corporate governance standards and guidelines. The *OECD Principles of Corporate Governance* were agreed in 1999 and are intended to assist member and non-member governments in their efforts to evaluate and improve the legal, institutional and regulatory framework for corporate governance in their countries, and to provide guidance and suggestions for stock exchanges, investors, corporations and other parties that have a role in the process of developing good corporate governance. However, it was also recognised that enterprises and countries needed to remain competitive in a changing world, and that governments have an important responsibility for shaping an effective regulatory framework that provides for sufficient flexibility to allow markets to function effectively and to respond to changing expectations. Thus the preamble to the Principles noted that they are evolutionary in nature and should be reviewed in light of significant changes in circumstances.

Since the Principles were agreed, activity in this area by member countries has surged. National principles, codes and review committees have proliferated and in some cases significant policy initiatives are either coming into place or are under consideration. A number of countries are also involved in reviewing their company law. The reasons for this activity are varied. In some cases the concern has been to "tweak" the system and to preserve, for example, competitiveness in capital markets. In these cases countries have sometimes chosen to use codes and principles put forward on a non-governmental basis. In other cases, corporate failures and scandals have called into question the veracity of published financial information and have placed governments under pressure to also take policy initiatives of a legal or regulatory kind. Yet the question remains whether these developments in member countries are sufficient to deal with both the immediate tensions and the longer term challenges, and whether the assumptions on which action is based are adequate. Against this background, the OECD Council Meeting at Ministerial Level in 2002 noted that the integrity of corporations, financial institutions and markets is essential to maintain confidence and economic activity, and to protect the interests of stakeholders. To maintain market integrity, the Ministers agreed to implement best practices in corporate and financial governance which "... entails an appropriate mix of incentives, balanced between government regulations and self-regulation backed by effective enforcement". To this end they agreed to survey developments and assess the Principles.

To meet this remit, the Steering Group on Corporate Governance agreed to prepare a synthesis paper covering major developments and associated issues in corporate governance and the lessons being learned, with the objective to establish a basis for assessing the Principles. To support the review, the OECD circulated a questionnaire to member countries together with a request to update the company law and corporate governance database. This paper presents preliminary results from this exercise, together with a survey of recent research and policy papers, which are serving to highlight key features of corporate governance arrangements.

The first chapter sets out the forces which are driving governments to reconsider governance arrangements, many of which were not long ago regarded as either excellent or at least as not presenting serious policy problems. Three key forces are identified. First, the strong stock market correction has exposed some systemic weaknesses with respect to audit and disclosure and thrown into question assumptions about how boards were carrying out their duties. The weaknesses have also contributed to financial market instability. Second, longer-run trends in both global and domestic financial markets are bringing corporate governance arrangements under pressure to adjust. Third, there is now a growing body of research confirming that corporate governance and financial market arrangements exert an important influence on growth prospects, a key policy concern. In thinking about policy responses, analysis and research have drawn attention to the need for better disclosure and transparency, the benefits of effective monitoring of management and the importance of investor rights. These factors are also key elements of the Principles. Nevertheless, the identification of specific measures should still take place within a policy framework which considers the relevant costs and benefits of proposed actions. In the corporate governance area, such analysis needs to take into account important connections between institutional features.

In responding to the policy challenges, governments face a broad choice of strategy in finding a balance between law, regulation and self-regulation as policy instruments. These issues are taken up in Chapter 2. The first subsection draws on information provided to update the OECD's company law and corporate governance database, which also includes a selective coverage of regulatory measures. The second subsection presents a broad oversight of the numerous principles and codes which are now in operation. Although many of these "voluntary" instruments are too recent for their effects to be clear, a growing literature investigating the compliance with, and the effectiveness of, past initiatives is briefly reviewed.

The third chapter presents a thematic review of recent developments and emerging issues. The sections follow the structure of the Principles, although the interlocking nature of the various elements is also emphasised. The first section covers the exercise of ownership rights including voting, protection of minority shareholders, the role of institutional investors and the importance of a market in corporate control. The second section covers stakeholders focusing on creditors and employees. Actions to increase transparency and disclosure, and to improve the incentive structures for auditors and analysts, are reviewed in the following section. The final section examines board issues including moves to introduce more "independence", the duties of the board including its audit functions, managing conflicts of interest, setting executive compensation, and promoting corporate ethics.

ISBN 92-64-10605-7
Corporate Governance: A Survey of OECD Countries
© OECD 2004

Chapter 1

Policy Concerns and Driving Forces

Immediate pressures on policy arise from corporate scandals and large failures...

Pressure on governments and on the business sector to improve corporate governance arrangements has arisen often in the context of the failure of large companies and particularly marked instances of corporate fraud (Box 1.1), and much the same has taken place since 2000. The spectacular collapse of Enron and Worldcom in the US and some companies in other countries has led to pressure and also action to change corporate governance practices. The essential difference between now and the past is that the international implications of problems which have come to light in the US have been marked, whereas past incidences in the UK, Australia, Japan etc. have mainly had national implications. Events in the US have led to uncertainty about the accuracy of information provided to financial markets world-wide, leading other countries to also re-examine their practices. The crisis in Korea in 1997 also involved corporate collapses. However, the impact on other OECD countries was primarily macroeconomic, acting through financial markets, and did not lead to a re-examination of corporate governance practices outside of Korea and Asia.

Bankruptcies, and borderline activities such as excessive perks for executives, are not necessarily a sign of governance weakness requiring policy action. To some extent bankruptcies are a cyclical phenomenon, especially in cycles characterised by booms either in bank financing or in the capital markets. This was true of Australia during the 1980s, Germany in the early 1990s with the reunification boom,[1] and especially true of the United States following the financial market euphoria at the end of the 1990s. The same thing would have occurred in Japan after the boom of the late 1980s, but the inevitable payback has been delayed by a limited bank safety net at first, and then by weak banking supervision, which promoted not a clean-up but forbearance.[2] Bubble periods have usually been characterised by phases when opportunities for quick profits seemed to multiply, leading in turn to business plans that in retrospect appear just short of fanciful. More importantly, incentives became distorted leading often to a breakdown in business ethics on the part of some, such as executives and accountants, who strove to "get their share". The corresponding bursting of a bubble serves to re-establish appropriate incentive structures and impart welcome discipline on issuers, investors and intermediaries. The experience does serve to highlight that the structure of incentives is an important feature of any governance system.

Box 1.1. **Large corporate collapses and the governance debate**

Large corporate failures have often stimulated debate about corporate governance, leading to regulatory action and other reforms. In the UK the collapse of the Maxwell publishing group at the end of the 1980s stimulated the Cadbury code of 1992, and cases through the 1990s such as Poly Peck, BCCI and recently Marconi stimulated a series of further enquiries and recommendations. Widespread distress among both banks and *chaebol* in Korea in 1997 was viewed as not only macroeconomic in origin but as also reflecting governance weaknesses. In Germany, the cases of Holtzman, Berliner Bank, and more recently Babcok have served the same catalytic role as did the collapse of HIH (a large insurer), Ansett Airlines and One Tel in Australia.* Crédit Lyonnais and Vivendi have raised many governance issues in France; and in Switzerland the events at Swissair have had a similar effect. Large failures of both financial and non-financial institutions in Japan have also led to regulatory responses and to legal changes. Finally, the cases of Enron, World Com and Tyco have initiated major debate and legislation in the US. At other times, large collapses (or near collapses) in some countries have either led to no systematic follow-up or to only some minor regulatory changes.

In thinking about these incidences of corporate failure, several features stand out. First, some cases are clearly related to bad business plans (even though *ex ante* they might have appeared visionary) and to poor managerial decisions. In some instances, government policy or informal pressure and regulatory forbearance have also been a contributing factor. Poor business plans and risk management have usually become apparent as macroeconomic conditions have tightened. However, in many of the cases cited above legitimate questions have arisen about the quality of the board (including the supervisory board in Germany) and whether it was in any position to exercise independent judgement. In addition, it has sometimes appeared that the board did not demand additional information from the management, but had actually almost become a part of it. Business failures might also be due to broader forces and not to corporate governance weaknesses. Thus from the macroeconomic viewpoint some companies will often need to go out of existence, the question being how efficiently the exit process works. In part this is determined by the efficiency of the bankruptcy system, but it is also related to timely decisions by the company which are related to its corporate governance arrangements. For example, in Germany and Japan massive over-capacity in the construction sector probably cannot be reduced without companies disappearing but in many cases the situation might have been handled in a more timely fashion.

Box 1.1. **Large corporate collapses
and the governance debate** (cont.)

Second, some collapses have involved fraud (in the everyday sense if not
the legal one) or the active cover-up and dissimulation by management, or
indeed both. Enron and Worldcom are recent examples of the two categories
and there is now a huge literature about these two cases. Maxwell, BCCI and
Polly Peck in the UK were similar. In many cases, the fraud or cover-up in
question was already illegal under existing statutes, and questions have
arisen about the quality of regulatory oversight (*e.g.* HIH in Australia, Enron in
the US). The most recent cases, but also some before, have in addition also
involved, by omission or commission, auditors and external lawyers of the
firm. But although sanctions were imposed in a number of cases, the problem
was not viewed as systemic.

Third, pension claims have emerged as a new feature of large collapses. The
Maxwell case in the UK involved the abuse of pension funds by dominant
directors. In Germany, Japan and in other countries where pension liabilities are
covered more or less by internal corporate provisions, incompetence or fraud
against the main firm will have the same effect of endangering pension assets.
The more recent failures (Enron in particular) have brought out another aspect,
which is the limited possibility at times for a pension scheme to diversify. The
mechanism includes lock-up provisions which force employees to continue to
hold the company's stock when prudence might indicate otherwise.

OECD member countries have also experienced a number of banking and
insurance failures during the past decade. Such cases have often led to
reviews of the regulatory system and to reform measures. In some instances
(*e.g.* the Savings and Loans collapse in the US) criminal charges have been
brought and successfully prosecuted. But apart from tighter monitoring of
the "fit and proper person" test for directors and major owners, the issue of
governance does not appear to have been pursued with the same vigour as in
the cases of non-financial collapses. However, this situation might now be
changing.

In sum, although financial and non-financial corporate failures cannot all
be attributed to corporate governance deficiencies, such weaknesses have
certainly played a role and contributed at least to the scale of the distress
which is of added importance now given the rising value of pension
liabilities. Weak corporate governance has been an important factor, and also
in the banking sector. In addition, the cases cited also pointed to the need to
review enforcement and regulatory oversight.

* For a discussion of collapses in Australia see *Collapse Incorporated*, CCH, Australia, 2001. For a
general overview of the pathology of crisis see G.P. Miller, *Catastrophic Financial Failures: Enron,
HIH and more*, Ross Parsons Lecture, Sydney 2002. Forthcoming in *Cornell Law Review*.

Corporate governance issues have also come to the fore recently in fully or partially state-owned companies in Europe (*e.g.* France, Germany, Italy, Belgium, Ireland, Greece, Sweden, Norway) and several years ago in Australia. In the EU, the state is still the largest direct or indirect shareholder in 45 out of 143 large privatised enterprises which sometimes represent a significant share of market capitalisation.[3] In some cases, governments have pursued their own objectives regardless of minority (in some cases quite large) shareholders, and control devices such as golden shares have been, at least until recently, important. Such actions serve to reduce the firm's future access to capital markets and also to distort the European single market. In addition, there is often a non-transparent budgetary cost. Although the extent of the problem is limited by tight monitoring of state aid rules by the European Commission, there is nevertheless a serious economic/political issue that remains to be solved.Similar issues arise in countries outside the EU even though they are not always viewed through the prism of potential distortion of competition.[4] The Steering Group has recently asked its Working Group on Privatisation and Governance of State-owned Assets to develop principles and best-practices on corporate governance of state-owned assets.

Financial market developments are also forcing the agenda

Deeper and more liquid international financial markets and new financial instruments have served to heighten awareness amongst policy makers of the need to continually update and review microeconomic structures, including arrangements regarding transparency and disclosure.[5] And indeed, this is what most governments have been doing through the latter half of the 1990s (see below), and especially since the Asian crisis in 1997. While deeper and more liquid financial markets do not necessarily imply the need for policy action with respect to governance *per se,* since markets could be expected to make their own contractual arrangements if needed, there is still a need for prudential oversight since incentives might sometimes get out of line. For example, some have been concerned about the potential for a "race to the bottom" in private regulatory arrangements. In the EU where national capital markets have been competing to establish their own credibility there is no evidence of such a development.[6] Competition to develop high-technology special listings in the late 1990s in both the EU and Japan has been seen as competition to lower standards by some. However, a closer examination suggests that this was less the case than a move to set standards suitable for venture and high growth companies (*e.g.* Neue Markt in Germany and MOTHERS in Japan) while leaving the standards for the main listing essentially unchanged.

An important feature of financial markets and corporate finance with implications for governance arrangements is the rise of institutional investors: financial assets of institutional investors have risen from 38 per cent of GDP in 1981 to 90 per cent in 1991 and to 144 per cent in 1999.[7] Acting as intermediaries, they are also the largest owner of domestic equity in a number of countries (see Table 1.1.B below). At the same time, the holding period for shares owned by some types of financial institution might not be very long and in many cases the institutions have proved to be passive shareholders; for the mutual fund industry in the US, turnover has increased from around 30 per cent in the 1980's to around 100 per cent in recent years implying that the holding period has decreased from over three years to just under a year.[8] One of the reasons for the rapid growth of institutional shareholders is that they are a response to the demand by individual investors for portfolio diversification and greater liquidity, not to mention the desire by investors to equal or "beat the market average". It is often argued that, as large investors, they might have an important role to play in corporate governance by monitoring companies and by taking a more active ownership role rather than remaining a passive investor (see below). The question is even more pertinent now when expectations of reasonable absolute returns might need to involve investor pressure on management for better performance. The decision is up to the institution involved but the capacity for manoeuvre is not always open. In a number of countries, pension funds and other institutional investors (including individuals) are restricted in their activities and in reducing monitoring costs by pooling information and communicating with each other about their voting intentions.[9] However, the argument for greater activism does suppose that the intermediaries are themselves subject to appropriate corporate governance regimes and that there are no conflicts of interest with other shareholders.[10] Many of these issues remain to be resolved and are considered in more depth in Chapter 3.

Rising pension savings have underpinned the growth of institutional investors including insurance companies. To meet the challenges of ageing, almost all countries have introduced structural policies to encourage and facilitate the accumulation of private pension savings by either companies or individuals, and bargaining between the social partners has often led to the establishment of what are now large and maturing corporate schemes. In some instances, reserves for public pension liabilities (e.g. Ireland) have also been established. Such developments have a number of implications for governance arrangements. First, company funds or reserves might need to be better secured. The UK was arguably the first to suffer large scale abuse of captive pension funds in the late 1980s (i.e. the Maxwell case). The Enron case is somewhat different and is representative of a number of other firms where pension funds have been invested mainly in the company and employees have been limited in their ability to sell their holdings of the company's equity. In such schemes the company has usually also made a contribution of the company's shares with restrictions on individuals in their rights to sell the shares or diversify their portfolios. Second, pension commitments and the associated employees and retirees are growing in stature as a major claimant alongside other creditors and shareholders.

In several countries (*e.g.* Germany, Japan, Korea, Austria) banks (and in some cases also insurance companies) have had an important place in the overall corporate governance system, serving both a monitoring and a financial role, but this system is now weakening.[11] Bank financing and shareholding have served to underpin stakeholders such as management and, indirectly, employees. This has led to the categorisation of these corporate governance systems as bank-dominated and insider controlled. There is now a vast literature concerning whether financial and governance systems are in the process of converging or whether the influence of the past will remain dominant (*e.g.* path dependence).[12] It is not, however, necessary to take an explicit position in this debate in order to highlight several public policy issues, which arise from a general weakening in the financial and competitive position of banks in these countries. For example, the large universal banks in Germany have been retreating from their special relationship with enterprises in a bid to retain profitability. New insider trading rules might also serve to reduce the private returns from their monitoring activities, although the law can also be seen as reacting to developments rather than as leading them.[13] In Japan, banks are burdened by weak balance sheets and have been under pressure since the 1970s from alternative sources of corporate finance – and many successful companies have never been associated with a main bank. The banks are now required to reduce their corporate shareholdings to at least 100 per cent of their Tier I capital. If, as seems likely, corporate governance systems are characterised by strong mutual support between major institutional features, there is a danger that a reduced role or capability for banks might weaken the overall system unless new institutional forms arise either spontaneously, or are made possible through policy initiatives. In Germany it is not yet evident that a replacement for the monitoring activities of the banks is evolving and this is also the case in Japan, despite recent changes to the corporate law. Bank governance[14] is also an important issue in Japan, Korea, Mexico and Turkey although in the former two countries a number of measures have recently been taken.[15]

And the objective to promote growth is focusing attention on corporate governance

In recent years, policy has come to emphasise the need to improve growth and this has led to greater emphasis on measures to ease the assimilation of new technologies and the promotion of entrepreneurship, both of which are broadly related to corporate governance arrangements.[16] Research by the OECD underpins the importance of investment, human capital formation, R&D and innovation for the growth process. While in some countries the rapid development of a few new sectors such as Information and Communications Technology (ICT) has driven growth, more generally the bulk of productivity gains comes from the developments in existing sectors with the role of entry and exit markedly different between countries.[17] The major policy lesson drawn by the OECD study is that attention needs to be focused on getting the fundamentals right: promoting competition which leads in turn to innovation and R&D, and improving the functioning of product, labour and financial markets. The importance of financial markets is supported at both the macroeconomic and microeconomic level: financial development is related to economic growth per capita and total factor productivity through its influence on fixed investment and by other channels such as better resource allocation. Among the different indicators of financial development investigated, stock market capitalisation and private credit issued by deposit money banks had a statistically significant affect on growth.[18] Others have already stressed the relationship between financial development and legal and other infrastructure, which is also a key component of corporate governance.[19] At the microeconomic level, the study also noted the importance of resources moving between enterprises and the pattern of company entry and exit, both of which are related to financial development.[20]

Beyond the observation that financial market development is related to key governance institutions such as investor protection, the broader relationship between governance arrangements and growth, while well known from theory, has been difficult to discover in practice.[21] There are a number of reasons why the macroeconomic relationship is difficult to determine. First, it is not clear what should be the object of focus. Growth rates may be less affected by governance arrangements than the likelihood of crisis, which can prove very costly to the level of income per capita. Even though crisis prevention is often the object of policy concern – and has driven the recent emphasis on governance arrangements – it has not figured greatly in empirical work in the OECD area.[22] Second, apart from the difficult issue of specifying all other relevant determinants of growth for empirical work, it is not clear how governance arrangements should be represented at the national or macroeconomic level. Structural indicators of governance such as those developed by the OECD for labour and product markets remain under-developed. Governance arrangements also need to be considered as endogenous (Box 1.2), which is why studies usually focus on broader systemic features such as the type of legal system and measures of formal shareholder rights. Such indicators are, however, difficult to interpret from a policy perspective and do not represent adequately what actually happens in a country's corporate system. The latter will also depend on the sector and size distribution of companies.

Box 1.2. **Corporate governance arrangements are also evolving in response to new circumstances**

As economies evolve it is important that corporate governance arrangements are able to adjust. The policy framework has changed greatly in a number of member countries including reforms of the tax system, strengthening competition through regulatory reform and the promotion of venture capital. In some cases, labour market flexibility has also been enhanced. Directly or indirectly these initiatives might have implications for corporate governance arrangements although the need for a policy response is not obvious. For example, the OECD has found that increased product market competition serves to reduce the rents available for distribution to insiders and this will place insider-dominated governance systems under pressure to adjust. Governance arrangements might evolve more or less spontaneously without much need for policy measures beyond facilitating the process. Two examples concern accounting standards and company law.

The rapid growth of human capital intensive companies and industries can be expected to change the way in which companies are governed or at least the balance of factors that will be taken into account when reaching decisions. But the changes to governance arrangements will also depend on whether, for example, the founder is still in control or whether the firm is more mature and in the hands of professional management. Thus to attract talent and to retain firm specific human capital, high tech companies have often resorted to heavy use of stock options which have, in some cases, resulted in dilution of existing shareholders interests. Since such options have often been constructed in such a way that they did not need to be expensed, the implications for shareholders have not been entirely clear. If the expense related to option grants is recognised, which is to a great extent a regulatory question, the balance between the interests of the insiders and outsiders may have to be more clearly established.[1] Another illustration of the facilitating role of regulation concerns Japan. To allow private governance arrangements for start-ups to give a greater voice to founding financiers required changes to the Japanese corporate codes.[2]

1. For a controversial view which is based on the fact that non-expensed options accounted for a great deal of the measured profits during the latter part of the 1990s, see J. Plender, *Going Off the Rails*, Wiley 2003.
2. *OECD Economic Survey of Japan*, 2001.

There is now a body of research, which taken together points to a key role for fundamental aspects of corporate governance in improving performance. They include shareholder and creditor protection, enforcement, transparency and accountability. There are two types of studies. The first focus on measures of individual company performance, either within or between countries

(Box 1.3). For the former, a large study indicates that agency costs for shareholders *vis-à-vis* management are significant but can be dealt with. Other studies go further, indicating an important role for board composition, not necessarily with respect to restricted indicators of performance such as profitability, but in controlling risk (see Box 3.5 below). The cross country studies indicate how important it is to protect minority shareholders and creditors in the most general situation in the OECD area of dominant owners, especially where such owners exercise control in non-transparent ways. A number of limitations related to these studies are also clear. In particular, none of the studies examine the role of labour as a stakeholder even though in several countries employees are represented on the board and in even more countries employment protection legislation reinforces and legitimises their position as a stakeholder. The degree of product market competition has also been neglected. More importantly, however, is the difficulty of extrapolating from enterprise performance to macroeconomic performance. This relationship is better approached by the sector studies.

The second set of studies, which focus on inter-sector growth rates, indicate a direct relationship between the aspects of corporate governance associated with financial development and growth. To summarise a large and growing empirical literature, "… there is a clear association between different financial and corporate systems and types of economic activity … although there is not necessarily a dominant financial and corporate system that is appropriate to all economies or all industries within an economy".[23] Market oriented systems and high ownership concentration favour high skill industries, more R&D and a more efficient use of capital. Underpinning these features are clear accounting standards (and, by implication, transparency) and protection of shareholder rights, particularly minority shareholders.[24]

The present focus among policy-makers on the link between corporate governance arrangements and growth has, together with an increasing volume of analytical and empirical research, advanced the prospects of developing an analytical framework that may provide guidance in policy design. The advantages of such policy making tools is that they would be adaptable to differing legal and regulatory frameworks and would present a coherent focus on *desired economic outcomes* rather than be returns from specific corporate governance provisions in isolation.

Implications of the forces at work for policy

Although the unwinding of financial market excesses of the late 1990s should realign incentive structures in favour of improved governance behaviour, recent experience has exposed structural or systemic weaknesses in corporate governance arrangements that might not simply go away.

CORPORATE GOVERNANCE: A SURVEY OF OECD COUNTRIES – ISBN 92-64-10605-7 – © OECD 2004

Box 1.3. **Governance and economic performance: empirical evidence at the firm level**

Studies using what are considered to be best practice econometric techniques indicate that corporate governance is an important determinant of performance. Establishing an empirical relation between corporate governance and performance is exceedingly difficult since there is a considerable leeway in specifying measures of performance and indicators of corporate governance are very restricted. It is not possible at present to use a widely accepted index of overall corporate governance.[1] As with all regression work, the question of "causality" will never be resolved fully to everybody's satisfaction, in part because of poor measurement, and the implications for practical policy are sometimes difficult to interpret. Nevertheless, best practices have emerged that address many of the issues and usually involve examining a panel of companies over time using quite specific aspects or features of governance. Several of these state of the art studies are summarised here.[2]

One study focuses on differences in governance arrangements regarding take-overs which have the effect of strengthening management (and other stakeholders) vis-à-vis shareholders. Gompers, Ishii and Metrick[3] use a time series extending over the 1990s for around 1 500 firms per year. Contrary to what is often perceived abroad, as in Europe the United States is very heterogeneous with respect to take-over defences with a number of states extending the possibility for substantial protection of management, and in a number of cases also for other stakeholders.[4] They find a striking relationship between corporate governance and stock returns since an (ex post) investment strategy that bought firms with the strongest shareholder rights and sold firms with the weakest rights would have earned abnormal returns of 8½ per cent per year over the 1990s. The result is robust with respect to sub-periods and to industrial composition of the firms, thereby taking into account any "distortion" due to the boom in stock prices of high technology companies at the end of the 1990s. Moreover, there is also a relationship between valuation and their measure of governance: a one point worsening of their governance index is associated with a 2.4 percentage point lower value for Tobin's Q (the ratio of market value to replacement costs of an enterprise) and at one point at the end of the 1990s it even rose to some 9 per cent. How did poorer governance lead to such differences? The authors find that poorer governance in the sense of reduced shareholder rights is associated with inferior levels of operating performance as well as with greater capital expenditure and acquisition activity. The latter matches other research pointing to the fact that a large number of acquisitions do not benefit the acquiring company. It would seem from their results that the reduced effective monitoring capacity of shareholders could lead to greater agency costs in the form of management pursuing other objectives such as expansion via acquisitions, inefficient investments, etc.

Box 1.3. **Governance and economic performance:
empirical evidence at the firm level** (cont.)

Some caution is, however, necessary even though the results are apparently robust. The estimates refer to fixed effects, so that the regressions do not explain variation between firms. Yet from the viewpoint of policy, the question often comes down to knowing which firm specific arrangements improve performance. Put another way, they did not estimate what would happen if a company decided to improve (reduce) shareholder power since other governance measures such as changes in shareholder concentration or board composition were not investigated at the same time (see Börsch-Supan and Köke). It is therefore difficult to draw a simple policy conclusion that just changing take-over laws would, *ceteris paribus*, improve performance. But it is nevertheless an important result. One aspect is, however, intriguing and is relevant for policy: it would appear that investors were surprised by the relative performance of the two groups of companies, otherwise market prices would have adjusted. Have investors learned? That is an important question if instruments such as "comply or explain" are to be effective in changing incentives and therefore corporate behaviour.

As with a great deal of the empirical corporate governance literature a key question is whether the general result for the US, that agency costs matter, extends to other countries with an even greater range of institutions (*i.e.* the general proposition that regardless of system, agency costs matter). Two recent studies appear to support the general importance of agency costs by examining the protection of minority shareholders and creditors as well as the role of large shareholders (subject to some important caveats), ownership forms that are prevalent in most of the non-US/UK OECD area.

A study by Gugler *et al.*[5] used a form of Tobin's Q comparing the average rate of return on investment to a firm's cost of capital which included a sector specific depreciation rate to account for technological change, R&D and advertising which typically varies by industry. This dependent variable has the advantage of picking up excess investment, which might be a problem in regimes with poor corporate governance, and in reducing the role of market measures of corporate value. Investment includes R&D and advertising expenditures which can produce intangible capital. A potential weakness of the study is the unavoidable use of an average rate of return on investment instead of the theoretically more appropriate marginal rate. The sample comprises 19 000 firms in 61 countries over the period 1985-2000, although the sample with ownership data was much smaller and the time period more restricted. The ownership variables included shareholding by management, the extent of cross shareholding by other firms, and the extent of pyramiding including the deviation of cash flows from voting

Box 1.3. **Governance and economic performance: empirical evidence at the firm level** (cont.)

rights. On average, only around 30 per cent of firms have ownership structures with no deviation of cash flow from voting rights. In brief, they found evidence of agency problems in all countries with significant effects on investment performance, although institutions could mitigate the costs incurred. Key conclusions are: i) Differences in investment performance were related more to the legal system than to ownership structure. Without an appropriate legal system, neither control by another non-financial company nor a financial firm improved performance. ii) To be effective in reducing agency costs, dominant shareholders including families need to be counter-balanced by protection for minority shareholders. iii) At least in the US, shareholding by management up to around 25 per cent improved performance but above this level it deteriorated, suggesting the occurrence of management entrenchment. iv) External capital markets and strong creditor protection improved performance. v) Good accounting standards exercised an important influence on behaviour almost regardless of other factors.

Finally, a study by La Porta *et al.*[6] seeks to examine the effect on corporate value of shareholder protection in the context of a controlling shareholder. The latter can improve value by reducing agency costs but it can also lead to exploitation of minority shareholders through mechanisms such as transactions not at arms length (sometimes called tunnelling).[7] This is particularly likely when the cash flow rights of the dominant shareholder differs from the control rights by, for example, pyramiding. The study focuses on a sample of 539 large firms in 27 predominantly OECD economies. The dependent variable is Tobin's Q and the authors control for sales growth thereby trying to separate any effects due to sectoral composition. Although there are econometric problems with separating the effect of cash flow ownership from control, the results do suggest that poor shareholder protection is associated with lower valuations and that high cash flow ownership by the controlling shareholder improves valuation, especially where shareholder protection is poor. Control rights greater than cash flow rights, an issue in Europe, might lead to expropriation of minority shareholders.

1. Some studies are now using aggregate indicators with interesting results although the weighting of individual elements, and the key assumption of whether they stand in a complementary or substitute relationship with each other, remains untested. For one study using an aggregate index at the firm level and which found that better corporate governance lowered the cost of capital see W. Drobetz, A. Schillhofer and H. Zimmermann, "Corporate governance and expected stock returns: evidence from Germany", *ECGI Finance Working Paper*, 11/2003.

> ## Box 1.3. **Governance and economic performance: empirical evidence at the firm level** (cont.)
>
> 2. Börsch-Supan and Köke stress the importance of using panel data (a cross section of firms or countries over time) and to control for missing variables which might otherwise lead to the problem of spurious correlation. Among those they note are often excluded is the degree of product market competition. But for econometric studies to be effective, it must also be possible to observe differences in governance arrangements, however defined. Measuring corporate performance is not as straight forward as measuring aggregate economic performance. Poor governance arrangements might actually be reflected in rapid growth for a period as firms embark on mergers and acquisitions and on expansion plans. In these circumstances the relevant variable to measure corporate performance includes accounting profits, market value or the growth rate of market value and return on assets. Some also include preconditions for profits such as the number of patents produced. Unfortunately, the correlation between these measures is low so that results may depend on the endogenous variable chosen. In any case, errors in measuring the endogenous variable (what it is that needs to be explained) may lead to spurious, insignificant and unusable estimation results. A. Börsch-Supan and J. Köke, "An applied econometrician's view of empirical corporate governance studies", *German Economic Review*, 3(3), 2002.
> 3. P. Gompers, J. Ishii and A. Metrick, "Corporate Governance and Equity Prices"; NBER *Working Paper*, 8449, 2001.
> 4. For example, some states prohibit an acquirer from using any surplus cash in the pension fund of the target to finance an acquisition. Thirty one states have laws allowing a widening of directors' duties providing boards with the legal basis for rejecting a take-over that would have been beneficial to shareholders. In two states the laws are explicit that the claims of shareholders should not be held above other stakeholders. See references contained in Annex A. of Gompers *et al.*
> 5. K. Gugler *et al.*, "Corporate governance, capital market discipline and the returns on investment", *Wissenschaftszentrum Berlin Discussion Paper*, FS IV 01-25, 2001.
> 6. R. La Porta *et al.*, "Investor Protection and corporate valuation", *The Journal of Finance*, June 2002.
> 7. Tunnelling is defined as the transfer of assets and profits out of firms for the benefit of their controlling shareholders and has been observed in the past in Belgium, France, the Czech Republic and Italy. See S. Johnson *et al.*, "Tunnelling", *NBER Working Paper*, 7523, 2000. It is also discussed in a country context in *OECD Economic Survey of Belgium*, 2003.

Moreover, in view of the present level of uncertainty and challenges to the legitimacy of the system of management,[25] it is prudent to review corporate governance arrangements to see if they have worked in the way expected and, if circumstances have changed, what adaptations are required. In some countries the areas of contention are more or less well defined (*e.g.* improved board oversight of conflicts of interest, better disclosure arrangements, tighter enforcement) even though the extent of required measures might remain in dispute. For a larger number of OECD countries, however, the pressures at work are less clear but the absence of spectacular company failures does not indicate that all is necessarily well. The price of inaction is likely to be reduced opportunities for growth.

A heterogeneous corporate landscape (Box 1.4) and the different nature of the recent business cycle in each country means that the corporate governance agenda varies between them. In a large number of OECD countries, controlling shareholders predominate which can be a positive feature serving to reduce agency costs (costs associated with management

Box 1.4. **The corporate landscape in the OECD area remains heterogeneous**

It is commonly accepted that the structure of ownership in the US and the UK is widely dispersed while in other countries the situation is one of concentrated ownership. This picture is, however, somewhat exaggerated. While the median largest voting block in these two countries is 10 per cent or less and 30-60 per cent in other countries (Table 1.1.A), there are also a number of companies with very concentrated voting power as shown in the maximum column and by the relatively large difference between the median and the mean. As in other countries these companies often reflect the dominance of a family holding. Much the same pattern emerges when considering the second and third largest voting blocks, with the UK rather more similar to Europe than to the US.

The identity of the shareholders also differs widely in the OECD with financial institutions important in the countries reported with the exception of France (Table 1.1.B). The nature of the institution is also different with pension funds very important in the US and the UK. The importance of banks in Japan needs to be seen against the background that insurance companies are their major shareholders. With respect to the non-financial sector, individuals are dominant in the US but in most other countries, except the UK, it is other companies. This clearly reflects the operation of company groups in many countries.

Groups of companies are often associated with particular control devices such as pyramids and cross shareholdings. One study examined 2 890 companies in Europe finding that nearly 30 per cent of them were in the third or lower down layers but that a third also showed no deviation of cash flow from voting rights. The lowest deviation for the average cash to voting rights ratio was in the UK while there were large deviations in Belgium, France and Germany, with a rather complex picture emerging for Italy.

In Italy the governance system is characterised by voice rather than by exit of the important shareholders. Powerful families, financial holding companies and cross shareholdings are a common feature. Corporate networks, voting agreements and hierarchical groups, especially in Belgium, France and Italy, are a device for concentrating voting power without concentrating ownership and cash flow rights.* They also shield the controlling group from hostile take-overs. However, they also open the system to abuse of minority shareholders.

* A. Melis, "Corporate governance in Europe: an empirical analysis of the Italian case", *Working Paper Universita di Cagliari*, 1998.

Table 1.1. **The varying corporate landscape**
A. The predominance of voting blocks...

	No. of public companies	Largest voting block				2nd largest voting block				3rd largest voting block				4-10th largest voting block			
		Min.	Med.	Mean	Max.	Min.	Med.	Mean	Max.	Min.	Med.	Mean	Max.	Min.	Med.	Mean	Max.
Austria	50	10.0	52.0	54.1	100.0	0.0	2.5	7.8	34.0	0.0	0.0	2.6	21.0	0.0	0.0	1.1	11.2
Belgium	140	8.4	56.0	55.9	99.8	0.0	6.3	10.3	44.3	0.0	4.7	4.5	18.3	0.0	4.7	4.7	18.3
Germany	372	0.0	57.0	49.6	100.0	0.0	0.0	2.9	45.2	0.0	0.0	0.6	32.0	0.0	0.0	0.5	24.0
Spain	193	5.0	34.5	40.1	98.0	0.0	8.9	10.5	36.1	0.0	1.8	3.5	24.3	0.0	0.36	3.3	22.7
France	CAC40	0.0	20.0	29.4	72.7	0.0	5.9	6.4	19.7	0.0	3.4	3.0	8.5	0.0	0.0	0.5	7.1
Italy	214	2.1	54.5	52.3	100.0	0.0	5.0	7.7	34.0	0.0	2.7	3.5	26.4	0.0	0.0	5.1	45.4
Netherlands	137	0.0	43.5	42.8	99.9	0.0	7.7	11.4	58.5	0.0	0.0	4.0	44.9	0.0	0.0	4.4	43.7
Sweden	304	1.6	34.9	37.6	93.4	0.6	8.7	11.2	41.2	0.2	4.8	5.6	27.9	0.0	1.3	1.8	15.5
United Kingdom	207	3.4	9.9	14.4	78.9	3.0	6.6	7.3	26.3	3.0	5.2	6.0	25.7	3.0	3.9	4.1	10.1
United States																	
NYSE	1 309	0.0	5.4	8.5	92.9	0.0	0.0	3.7	40.1	0.0	0.0	1.8	25.0	0.0	0.0	0.9	15.6
Nasdaq	2 831	0.0	8.6	13.0	99.5	0.0	0.0	5.7	48.8	0.0	0.0	3.0	24.1	0.0	0.0	1.6	22.1

Source: Barca, F. and M Becht (eds.) (2001), The Control of Corporate Europe, OUP, Oxford, p. 318.

Table 1.1. **The varying corporate landscape** (*cont.*)

B. ... and different ownership structure

Ownership of common stock

Per cent at year end

	United States (1996)	Japan (2001)	Germany (1996)	France (1994)	United Kingdom (1994)	Italy (1994)	Sweden (1996)	Australia (1996)	Korea (1996)
Financial sector	46	40	30	8	68	8	30	37	26
of which:									
Banks and other financial institutions	7	30	10	4	10	5	1	4	12
Insurance companies and pension funds	28	10	12	2	50	3	14	25	6
Investment funds	12	0	8	2	8	0	15	8	8
Non-financial sector	54	60	70	92	32	92	70	63	74
of which:									
Non-financial enterprises	0	22	42	58	1	25	11	11	21
Individuals	49	20	15	19	21	50	19	20	34
Public authorities	0	1	4	4	1	8	8	0	7
Foreign	5	18	9	11	9	9	32	32	12
Total	100	100	100	100	100	100	100	100	100

Note: Due to rounding, these figures may not add up to the total. Pension funds in Japan are managed by trust banks and insurance companies. Division between banks and insurance companies are estimated. No data is available on the extent to which mutual funds own shares. Security houses do manage such funds. These companies are included under other financial institutions. Australian figures are for the end of September 1996.

Source: M. Maher and T. Andersson, *op. cit*, and updates by the OECD.

pursuing their own interests) and aligning incentives with other shareholders. However, without effective legal and institutional protection for minority shareholders and creditors, growth reducing behaviour might be encouraged and this could be made worse if other traditional sources of governance such as banks are in decline. The corporate governance agenda for these countries may therefore be quite different from others where, for instance, a major issue would be how to cope effectively with the rise of institutional investors. On the other hand, virtually all member countries need to deal with the ongoing forces of ageing, technological and financial change, and the changing structure of interest groups within enterprises as the importance of human capital resources increase.

Especially in the United States, but also in some other countries such as Australia, France, the Netherlands and Germany, recent problems have cast doubt on the accuracy of financial information being given to boards and released to the markets as financial statements. Questions have therefore been raised about the integrity of the financial markets.[26] Criticism has focused on internal and external audit procedures, accountancy standards and the potential for conflict of interest on the part of both auditors and of financial analysts who are employed by financial conglomerates. For example, the British financial services regulator (FSA) has found a positive correlation between a financial enterprise undertaking placements and other financial work for a company with a positive recommendation of that company by its analysts, suggesting that the opinion might be biased. This is also an issue in the United States. Accountancy standards, rules covering whether external auditors should be restricted in their ability to perform non-audit work (such restrictions are already in force in Japan, the United States, Netherlands and France, and under discussion in Germany) and arrangements covering activities by analysts are all areas requiring attention. Developments are reviewed in more detail below. In addition, arrangements covering company oversight of external audits and the internal accounting and risk management systems also need to be re-examined. Indeed, concern to improve information released to financial markets has driven a number of European countries to introduce corporate governance measures over the past 2-3 years (see below) and in the decision by the EU to adopt international, principles-based, accounting standards from 2005. Australia is also following suit. Nevertheless, although the problems concerning transparency might be clear and readily accepted, it is still an open question about whether they are in fact simply symptoms of more fundamental governance issues.

At a deeper level, experience in both the US and Australia (and perhaps now in France and Switzerland), and echoing the 1990s experience in other countries such as the UK and Germany (see Box 1.1), appears to point toward the lack of "independence of mind" on the part of some directors who often appear to have gone along with management. In many instances it appears that they have been less involved in wrongful actions than in failing to question the business plan or strategy of the company, and especially the advisability of euphoric expansion plans (both the United States and Australia). As these corporate plans are often the preserve of management (in some countries such as Italy also of block holders), the focus has in turn shifted to whether the compensation schemes offered to management (especially in the US, Australia, UK and now Germany) have in fact been compatible with the interests of shareholders – and indeed other stakeholders. Preliminary work indicates that this was not the case with the evidence pointing to the use of management power in negotiating remuneration packages leading to a misalignment of incentives.[27] In some countries such power might be more apparent from highly restrictive dismissal provisions. The reasons for "market failure" in determining executive compensation include the widespread use of compensation consultants and the desire by firms to pay above the average as a signalling device. These features are important when considering policy options. While executive compensation is often a serious political and equity issue (and with important overtones for legitimacy), an even more important consideration is what the incentive structure did to possibly distort resource allocation. The misalignment of incentives has been a major factor behind the push to expand earnings and share prices through excessive merger and acquisition activity, which in a number of cases has left firms over-leveraged.

In sum, OECD countries face a wide range of policy challenges including improved transparency and disclosure, better monitoring by boards and improved shareholder rights. Such features have already been identified in the Principles as key to an effective corporate governance system suggesting that implementation and enforcement need to be greatly improved.

Notes

1. In the case of Germany, the reunification boom led to significant speculative activity in the housing and construction sectors. The collapse of the civil construction company Holtzman and the near collapse of the state-owned Berliner Bank were in great measure a natural reaction to the boom, even though they have led quite correctly to government action to improve governance arrangements which were also clearly a contributing factor.

2. See *OECD Economic Survey of Japan*, various issues. As noted in the 2002 *Survey*, a new corporate law makes some reforms and there are groups in Japan now advocating further and deeper measures.

3. In France, four large privatised companies account for 20 per cent of market capitalisation of the Paris bourse and the comparable figure for the Milan exchange is 36 per cent.

4. The OECD takes this wider view in the country *OECD Economic Surveys*.

5. For a discussion of the role of these structural policies in influencing financial markets and the framework for monetary policy see *Turbulence in Asset Markets: The role of Micro Policies*, G10 Deputies, September 2002.

6. For example, although somewhat dated, see E. Wymeersch, "Convergence or divergence in corporate governance patterns in Western Europe", in J. McCahery *et al.*, ed., *Corporate governance regimes: Convergence and diversity*, Oxford, 2002.

7. *OECD Institutional Investors Statistical Yearbook 2001*.

8. The booming stock market at the end of the 1990s might have contributed to a shorter holding period as funds sought to realise book profits. Whether this pattern will now reverse is unclear at this stage with one observer believing that important structural changes in the way funds are operated might first be necessary. J. Bogle, *The Mutual Funds Industry in 2003: Back to the Future*, *www.vanguard.com/bogle_site/sp20030114.html*.

9. It might not be economic for any one investor to monitor closely a firm but to free ride on another which will result in too little monitoring overall. There are many private contractual arrangements that might mitigate this problem, but only as long as the regulatory framework is permissive. For example, amendments to the company act in Canada in 2001 included provisions to facilitate communication among shareholders. These remove unnecessary obstacles to the exchange of views by shareholders and others concerning management performance and initiatives presented for a vote by shareholders. The definition of "solicit" now excludes public pronouncements about how one is going to vote and reasons for that decision, and communications for the purpose of obtaining support for a shareholder proposal. In countries with mandatory bids such as the UK, there are also restrictions on acting as a group though the British authorities now have special regulations covering joint discussions between shareholders where the purpose is not to obtain control of the company. The SEC in the US has similar exceptions which are additionally concerned to avoid market manipulation.

10. For an indication of some of the issues involved see T. Woidtke, "Agents watching agents?: evidence from pension fund ownership and firm value", *Journal of Financial Economics*, 63, 2002.

11. The monitoring role of banks – a lynchpin of the insider or relational model – may not have been as straightforward as is implied in the earlier literature. For example, bankers and businessmen often sat on each others boards so that monitoring was not at arms length but more in the nature of a club. For documentation of this overlooked point M. Hellwig, *On the economics and politics of corporate finance and corporate control*, SSRN.

12. For example, R. Golson, "Globalising corporate governance", *Stanford Law School Working Paper*, 192, 2000.

13. In particular, the value of control rights in Germany (a proxy for private returns measured as the difference between voting and preferred stock prices) has fallen from around 30 per cent at the end of the 1980's to around 15 per cent late in the 1990's. For a discussion of the withdrawal of banks from monitoring see A. Hackethal, R. Schmidt and M. Tyrell, *Corporate governance in Germany: Transition to a modern capital market-based system?*, Paper prepared for the Conference on Corporate Governance: the Perspective of the New Institutional Economics, Sarrbrucken, October 2002.

14. For a review of the special features of bank governance, see Caprio, G. and R. Levine, *Corporate Governance of Banks: Concepts and International Observations*, Global Corporate Governance Forum, April 2002.

15. The OECD *Economic Survey of Japan,* 2002, called for the authorities to strengthen bank restructuring and to insist on reforms to governance and to operating structures including credit assessments. A programme announced in October 2002 strengthens the function of external auditors and puts banks on notice that the authorities will rigorously use their powers to issue a Business Improvement Administrative Order to a bank which has not achieved its rationalisation plan (for those which have been previously recapitalised). The government has also clarified the criteria under which it would convert preferential shares to normal voting shares. In Korea, the OECD *Economic Survey,* 2003, noted that the banks had returned to profitability and credit ratings have improved. However, despite government efforts to ensure independent and responsible management of the banks it owns, privatising them is essential to remove any doubts about government intervention in operational management decisions.

16. For a review see *The Growth Project: Beyond the Hype,* OECD, 2001.

17. *The Sources of Economic Growth in the OECD Countries,* OECD, 2003.

18. Leahy, M. *et al.,* "Contributions of financial systems to growth in OECD countries", *OECD Economics Department Working Papers,* 280, March 2001.

19. R. La Porta *et al.,* "Investor protection and corporate governance", *Journal of Financial Economics,* 58, 2000. However, the sample of this study is quite broad and it is not clear that a strong relationship might also apply only to OECD countries.

20. OECD, *op. cit.,* 2003 noted very different patterns of firm entry and exit across countries. New entrants in the US were much smaller in scale than European counterparts but when successful grew quite rapidly. The study hypothesised that the larger size in Europe led to a bias against innovative and risky activities while remaining agnostic about whether excessive dynamics might also be associated with economy-wide costs.

21. For an explanation of the theory underlying the relationship between corporate governance arrangements and growth see M. Maher and T. Anderson, "Corporate governance: Effects on firm performance and economic growth", in J. McCahery *et al., Corporate Governance Regimes: convergence and diversity,* Oxford, 2002.

22. For an exception see Johnson, *et al.,* who find that measures of corporate governance explain the extent of exchange rate depreciation and stock market decline during the Asian crisis better then do standard macroeconomic measures. S. Johnson *et al.,* "Corporate governance in the Asian financial crisis", *Journal of Financial Economics,* 58, 2000.

23. W. Carlin and C. Mayer, "How do financial systems affect economic performance", in J. McCahery *et al., Corporate Governance Regimes: Convergence and Diversity, op. cit.*

24. For an even stronger conclusion which argues that the evidence favours a greater reliance on equity finance see R. Rajan and L. Zingales, "Financial systems, industrial structure and growth", *Oxford Review of Economic Policy,* Vol. 17, 4, 2001.

25. For example, opinion polls show a dramatic fall in the standing of CEOs in the eyes of the public.

26. Concerns about lack of integrity were reflected in the record number of account restatements in the US during 2002. The steep decline of stock prices after 2000 should not be taken as *prima facie* evidence of lack of integrity since a macroeconomic correction to overvaluation was also underway.

27. The situation was made even worse by rapidly rising stock prices. But even without these, the incentive structure of remuneration systems, especially in the US, appears to have been deficient. One study concluded that "Whatever the appearances, executive compensation is not generally the product of arm's length bargaining, but is the result of a process that executives can substantially influence. Moreover, although executive compensation is set against the background of market forces, these forces are hardly strong enough to compel optimal contracting outcomes. As a result, executives can use their power to influence compensation arrangements and to extract rent". See L. Bebchuk, J. Fried and D. Walker, "Managerial power and rent extraction in the design of executive compensation", *NBER Working Paper*, 9068, 2002.

ISBN 92-64-10605-7
Corporate Governance: A Survey of OECD Countries
© OECD 2004

Chapter 2

Broad Policy Choices Underlying Recent Developments

Principles, regulation and law: a shifting balance

An important feature of the Principles is that they do not explicitly assign responsibility for implementation. Rather they are intended to serve as a reference point to be used by both policy makers as they deal with their legal and regulatory frameworks and by market participants as they develop their own practices. However, the preface does note that "as important a role as governments may play in shaping the legal, institutional and administrative environment in which corporate governance and control are developed, the main responsibility remains with the private sector". The efforts on the part of enterprises to improve their own corporate governance arrangements is only now becoming clearer with the development of indicators by a number of private bodies.

In dealing with corporate governance issues, member countries have used a varying combination of legal and regulatory instruments on the one hand, and voluntary codes and principles on the other. In some instances, the latter are backed by legal or regulatory obligations to "comply or explain". The balance between law, regulation and voluntary principles varies widely in the OECD area depending in part on history, legal traditions, efficiency of the courts, the political structure of the country and the stage of enterprise development. From the point of view of applied policy these factors are essentially given, but that should not prevent the current policy process from looking at alternatives when considering changes or new initiatives. In this regard, the principles developed by the OECD as part of its work on Regulatory Reform are useful. These principles call for policy initiatives to consider carefully the costs and benefits of the proposed changes and the consideration of a wide range of alternative policy instruments with the objective to minimise regulatory cost.[1]

Voluntary principles or codes delineate the direction for change while also allowing for the fact that "one size does not fit all" and that achieving the desired practice might be done via many different instruments and organisational structures. Compliance costs could thus be expected to remain lower than with regulatory alternatives. That said, most countries would also define some features such as basic financial information, transparency, etc., as legally binding. The variation within the OECD is wide. On the one hand, some countries take the view that "principles-based laws", supported by detailed best practice guidelines, is the preferred framework for governance issues. Moreover, setting out detailed requirements in regulations could lead

CORPORATE GOVERNANCE: A SURVEY OF OECD COUNTRIES – ISBN 92-64-10605-7 – © OECD 2004

to a "show me where it says we can't do it" mentality, with a shift in focus to complying with the rule rather than the policy behind it. A different approach can be found in Austria and Germany, with the former stating that there was no need for a set of principles since it is all covered in law and regulation. However, in Germany there is also a call to reconsider the nature and detail of corporate law. As Hommelhoff observes, the real issue is finding a pragmatic and reasonable balance between those issues that should be regulated by rule-makers outside the corporations – and by legislators and regulators – and those issues which should be left to the corporations' own regulation.[2]

There is also a greater tendency to devolve rule setting from the legislature to a regulator which in turn can choose between competing private groups to establish standards. This is the case in both the UK and in Germany where the listing regulator has accepted governance standards set by others, thereby restricting their voluntary nature but also lending them political legitimacy. The case of the two major US stock markets (NYSE, Nasdaq) is more difficult to classify. They have set their own standards, subject to SEC approval and oversight, but because they control most of the securities market they have established in effect a regulatory system.

A more recent pattern to emerge is a tightening of the enforcement of corporate law and regulation. This is particularly so in the United States where, for example, CEOs must now vouch for the accuracy of the financial statements making them potentially liable for the disclosure. In other countries such as Ireland, enforcement of corporate law has been tightened by focusing investigation and prosecution with a regulator separated from the line ministry, and Canada, like several other OECD member countries, has established a multi-agency white collar crime task force.

Corporate law and regulation

Even before recent events a number of countries (UK, Italy, Ireland) had been in the process of quite fundamental reviews of their corporate laws and a review is also underway in Switzerland. The reasons for such reviews include to "produce a cost effective, fair and transparent system that would balance the interests of business with those of shareholders, creditors and others", "improving competitiveness and favouring entrepreneurial activity", "an increased role for private ordering by corporate actors", and "greater protection for investors". In Ireland, it is intended that "… the reformed and streamlined company code should be effective, intelligible to company directors and shareholders, and that the law should reflect how business is actually transacted". In other countries, continuing changes in corporate organisation and finance have also led to important changes in corporate law (Japan, Germany, Finland, Turkey, Poland) and others are considering changes (Sweden, Portugal, Norway). Although corporate governance concerns may

Table 2.1. **Summary of recent changes to company law and regulation**

	Comply or explain with principles or codes	Defining audit functions and limits on auditors	Improving transparency	Defining and controlling conflicts of interest	Improving or easing voting. greater role for AGM	Role for independent directors
Belgium		+		+	+	+
United States		+	+	+		+
Spain	+	+	+	+		
Germany	+		+		+	
Austria		+				
Ireland		+				
Finland						
Portugal				+		
Netherlands	+	+	+		+	
Greece		+	+	+		+
Czech Republic		+	+	+	+	
Australia			+			
Turkey		+			+	
Poland	+	+	+	+		
Switzerland	+	+	+	+		+
United Kingdom			+			
Italy			+	+	+	+
Hungary						
Sweden					+	
Mexico	+		+			+
Korea			+	+	+	+
France			+		+	
Canada		+			+	
Japan		+	+		+	+
Denmark						
Slovak Republic						
New Zealand			+			
Norway						
Luxembourg						
Iceland						

+ indicates a recent (last year or two) legal or regulatory change.

Source: Country submissions to OECD and OECD Company law and corporate governance data base.

not have been paramount, at least initially in the process, recent changes to company law and regulations reflects the most recent concerns (Table 2.1). A number of countries have now taken legal measures to tighten audit functions and to improve transparency (see below). The need to protect minority shareholders against exploitation is also being tackled, including in Belgium and Italy where "tunnelling" has been an important problem.

Although the legal and regulatory reforms in the OECD appear to be heading in the direction of implementing the Principles, it would be useful to

CORPORATE GOVERNANCE: A SURVEY OF OECD COUNTRIES – ISBN 92-64-10605-7 – © OECD 2004

be able to summarise not just the direction of change but also the level of achievement or the starting point. Indeed, corporate governance research is slowly moving forward in this area leaving the easy to use civil law/common law distinction behind in favour of focusing on specific instruments. The OECD's Company Law and Corporate Governance data base is a valuable source of such information and after updates are completed from the recent questionnaire comparisons from 2000 to the end of 2002 will also be possible. However, summary statistics would need to be considered carefully since : i) they could not be computed simply by adding yes answers since some measures might be substitutes for others with different overall effects on corporate governance; ii) some features might not be considered explicitly in law or in regulation but via other more enabling instruments that would need to be identified; and iii) private arrangements and legal precedent might also have to be taken into account. A simpler exercise is to get some idea of the pattern of law and regulation in the OECD area. Preliminary tabulations will be presented at a later date.

The adoption of principles and codes

Since the Principles were agreed in 1999, some 30 codes or principles have been established in the OECD area, and if consideration is taken of voting codes by institutional investors and other similar sets of recommendations by specialised participants, the number is even greater. A summary of the principles currently in force in OECD countries is given in Table 2.2, together with their predecessors in order to give an idea about the direction of recent change. Several common features stand out. First, a large number of countries have been concerned to improve the operation of board supervision and more recently to improve the quality of board members.[3] Second, even in countries usually considered to be insider-oriented in corporate governance arrangements, there has been concern to improve the performance of companies and to secure their access to capital: growth issues appear to have had a role in setting the agenda. Third, improving accountability to shareholders has also been a motive, but this emphasis might have been more related to the nature of the sponsoring body. Fourth, there is a tendency to tighten the implementation of national principles by moving from being voluntary in nature to encompassing various interpretations of "comply or explain". Fifth, some national principles are in fact highly prescriptive and detailed.

Voluntary implementation or "comply or explain" provisions explicitly acknowledge that "one size fits all" is not an effective approach to corporate governance, but there is a great difference in how these provisions are implemented. In Germany, Spain and the UK, "comply or explain" has been included in the law which refers to the semi-official corporate governance

Table 2.2. **Summary of codes and principles in operation
and their predecessors**

Excluding specific principles such as those of investment funds

Nation	Code	Main objectives	Instruments
Australia	Australian Stock Exchanges (ASX) Corporate Governance Council, Principles of Good Corporate Governance and Best Practice Recommendations, March 2003.	Optimise individual performance to cope with a constantly changing environment.	Comply or explain principle required by ASX listing rules; balance of authority within the board, disclosure of the division of responsibility, professional competence of its members and ability to exercise independent judgement; separation of chair-CEO; establish board committees with majority independent directors; ethics oversight; greater shareholder involvement; transparent compensation tied to corporate and individual performance; protect whistleblowers.
	IFSA Corporate governance: a guide for fund managers and corporations, December 2002.	To promote improved company performance.	Comply or explain principle; requested CDIs voting on all material issues; competent and diversified board of majority-independent directors; chair an independent director; guidelines on executive remuneration and operation of audit committees; code of ethics required.
Austria	Austrian Code of Corporate Governance, September 2002.	Reinforce the confidence of investors and creating sustainable, long-term value.	One-share-one-vote principle; establish board committees, few independence requirements specified; transparent compensation tied to corporate and individual performance; conflicts of interest to be disclosed; minority shareholders representation in the supervisory board. Limits to holding multiple positions in supervisory. and management boards of different companies.
Belgium	Recommendations of the Federation of Belgian Companies (January 1998).	Improve companies' performance, competitiveness and/or access to capital.	Balance of authority within the board, which should comprise a number of non-executive directors; independence of committees.
	Cardon Report (December 1998).	Improve companies' performance, competitiveness and/or access to capital.	Comply or explain principle required by BSX listing rules; balance of authority within the board, which should comprise a number of non-executive and independent directors; transparent compensation tied to corporate performance.
Canada	Disclosure requirements and amended guidelines, Toronto Stock Exchange, March 2002	Improve the quality of corporate governance of Canadian corporations.	General acceptance of the Saucier Report, except the independent board leader as a listing requirement; disclosure of governance practices; shareholder approval of options plans.
	Beyond Compliance: building a governance culture (Saucier Report), November 2001.	Assist the competitive position of Canadian companies at home and abroad by strengthening governance practices.	Management supervision by the board of directors, which should comprise and be chaired by outside (non-executive) directors; establish audit committee with only outside directors.

CORPORATE GOVERNANCE: A SURVEY OF OECD COUNTRIES – ISBN 92-64-10605-7 – © OECD 2004

Table 2.2. **Summary of codes and principles in operation and their predecessors** (cont.)

Excluding specific principles such as those of investment funds

Nation	Code	Main objectives	Instruments
Czech Republic	Revised Corporate Governance Code, Czech Securities commission, February 2001.	To set out the best practice on transparency and accountability for companies in the Czech Republic in order to encourage investor confidence.	Boards' effectiveness and responsibility; equal treatment and protection of shareholders; transparency; active role of institutional investors; boards should act independently of majority shareholders; 25 per cent independent directors in the supervisory board; disclosure of any conflict of interest by directors; establish committees comprising a majority of independent directors.
Denmark	Nørby Report and Recommendations (December 2001).	Improve company performance, competitiveness and/or access to capital.	Full decision power to shareholders in case of takeover bid; quarterly reports recommended; management supervision by the board of directors; management pay proportional to corporate results and responsibilities assumed; board formed entirely of non-executive directors; staggered boards recommended.
	Danish Shareholders Association Guidelines (February 2000).	Improve accountability to shareholders and/or maximise shareholder value.	4 non-executive directors in the board; establish remuneration committee; transparent compensation tied to corporate performance.
Finland	Chamber of Commerce/ Confederation of Finnish Industry and Employers Code (February 1997).	Improve quality of board (supervisory) governance.	
	Ministry of Trade and Industry Guidelines (November 2000).	Improve companies' performance, competitiveness and/or access to capital.	
France	Pour un meilleur gouvernement des entreprises cotées (Bouton rapport), Septembre 2002.	Revision of the Viénot reports after recent company events.	Viénot reports as a starting point; board supervision of management; competent and diversified board with ⅓ to ½ independent directors; independence of external auditors; audit and compensation committees entirely of non-executive directors and with ⅔ independent directors; concern for balance-sheet volatility from the adoption of IAS accounting standards.
	Hellebuyck Commission Recommendations (June 1998; updated October 2001)	Improve accountability to shareholders and/or maximise shareholder value.	Improve shareholders' participation, information and voting at AGM; establish board committees with ⅓ – majority independent directors; transparent compensation tied to corporate performance.
	Viénot I and II Reports (July 1995 and July 1999)	Improve quality of board (supervisory) governance.	Pre-eminent role of the board and collegial nature of its decisions; establish board committees; at least ⅓ independent directors; audit committees made for ⅓ of independent directors.

Table 2.2. **Summary of codes and principles in operation
and their predecessors** (*cont.*)

Excluding specific principles such as those of investment funds

Nation	Code	Main objectives	Instruments
Germany	Berlin Initiative Code (GCCG) (June 2000).	Improve quality of board (supervisory) governance.	Voluntary. Balance of power within and between management and supervisory board; compensation tied to corporate performance and seniority; establish supervisory board committees; facilitate shareholders' voting.
	German Panel Rules (January 2000).	Improve accountability to shareholders and/or maximise shareholder value; improve board (supervisory) governance.	Voluntary. Provisions of German company and group law concerning shareholder protection, disclosure and transparency, boards' composition, responsibilities and remuneration.
	Cromme Commission Code (February 2002) Now the German Kodex updated May 2003.	To promote the trust of international and national investors in the management and supervision of listed German stock corporations.	Comply or explain principle in law; improved disclosure to shareholders and voting possibilities; establish supervisory board committees; transparent compensation tied to corporate performance and seniority; disclosure of directors' conflicts of interest.
Greece	Mertzanis Report (October 1999).	Improve companies' performance, competitiveness and/or access to capital.	Improve shareholders' participation, information and voting at AGM; board: separation between Chair and CEO, majority of non-executive directors, non specified number of independent directors; establish internal audit committee of at least three non-executive directors; compensation tied to corporate performance.
	Federation of Greek Industries Principles (August 2001)	Improve companies' performance, competitiveness and/or access to capital.	
Hungary	None.		
Iceland	None.		
Ireland	IAIM Guidelines (March 1999).	Improve quality of board (supervisory) governance.	Endorsement of UK Combined Code; establish remuneration committee; limits to share option schemes; compensation tied to corporate performance.
Italy	Corporate governance code, Borsa Italiana, revised, July 2002 (Preda code)	Improve company performance, competitiveness and/or access to capital; improve quality of governance-related information available to equity markets.	Voluntary comply or explain. Unspecified but sizable number of non-executive and independent directors; neutrality on separating CEO and Chair; executive committee full reporting duty to the board; establish remuneration committee with majority of non-executive directors; compensation tied to corporate performance; establish internal control committees, entirely made up by non-executive directors, a majority of whom independent; substantial and procedural fairness in transactions with related parties.

CORPORATE GOVERNANCE: A SURVEY OF OECD COUNTRIES – ISBN 92-64-10605-7 – © OECD 2004

Table 2.2. **Summary of codes and principles in operation and their predecessors** (cont.)

Excluding specific principles such as those of investment funds

Nation	Code	Main objectives	Instruments
Japan	Revised Corporate Governance Principles, Japan Corporate Governance Forum, October 2001.	Improve the development of sound corporate governance in Japan.	Voluntary. Compensation tied to corporate performance for directors and employees; separation CEO-Chair; majority of the board of outside directors; establish committees chaired and in majority of outside directors, independent directors for the audit committee.
Korea	Code of best Practice for Corporate governance, September 1999.	To maximize corporate value by enhancing the transparency and efficiency of corporations for the future.	Voluntary. Improve shareholders' participation, information and voting at AGM; at least ¼ outside directors;[1] cumulative voting to ensure representation of minority shareholders; establish committees, audit committee chaired and made of ⅔ outside directors; disclosure of all information material to shareholders' decision-making.
	Update February 2003.		Comply or explain for listing; different requirements for large and small firms; outside directors independent from controlling families; minimum number of such directors 2 with above a half for large firms; fair disclosure and greater role for outside directors in audit, etc.; institutions to exercise voting rights and disclose.
Luxembourg	None.		
Mexico	Código de Mejores Prácticas Corporativas, July 1999.	Improving the quality of the board; tightening audit functions, improve transparency.	At least 20 per cent outside directors[1] on the board; establish committees, the auditing committee chaired by an outside director; improve shareholders' participation, information and voting at AGM.
Netherlands	Peters Report (June 1997).	Improve quality of board (supervisory) governance.	Voluntary. Supervisory board: report conflicts of interest to chairman, limited number of directorships to be held by the same person, remuneration not tied to the company's results, committees neither recommended nor discouraged; deviations from one-share-one-vote principle admitted (notably in takeover bids); improve shareholders' participation and information.
	SCGOP Handbook and Guidelines (August 2001).	Improve accountability to shareholders and/or maximise Shareholder value.	Comply or explain principle recommended; improve (institutional) shareholders' participation, information and voting; restrictions to issuance of multiple-voting shares and to anti-takeover defenses; supervisory directors' remuneration not tied to the company's results.

Table 2.2. **Summary of codes and principles in operation
and their predecessors** (cont.)

Excluding specific principles such as those of investment funds

Nation	Code	Main objectives	Instruments
	Tabaskblatt Commission Recommendations, July 2003.	Improve implementation of the Peters Report. Modernise practices.	Comply or explain to be legal requirement. Covers single and two tier boards. Define responsibilities of the management board to include risk management and control. Protect rights of whistle-blowers. Limit on directorships held. Remuneration policy to be approved by shareholders and full individual disclosure. Control of conflict of interest. Supervisory board to have retirement rota and committees including audit and remuneration. Independence from management and sectional interest. Independence defined. Majority independent directors and separation of chairman/CEO for single board companies. Change in identity of company to be approved by shareholders. Full powers of depository receipt holders. Disclosure by institutional investors and a fiduciary duty for them.
New Zealand	Stock Exchange Principles, 2003.		Exchange listing requirement; comply or explain; third of board independent; must separate chairman and CEO.
Norway	Under preparation.		
Poland	Best Practices in Public Companies, July 2002.	Improve company performance, competitiveness and access to capital. Improve board quality. Improve value for shareholders and stakeholders.	Comply or explain. Protection of minority shareholders; improve shareholders' participation, information and voting; improved transparency; at least ½ independent supervisory directors.
	Gdansk Institute for Market Economics (GIME), The CG Code for Polish Listed Companies, June 2002.	Protecting minority shareholders.	Comply or explain principle recommended; at least two independent supervisory directors; restrictions to anti-takeover defences; improve shareholders' participation, information and voting.
Portugal	Securities Market Commission Recommendations (November 1999, Revised 2001).	Improve companies' performance, competitiveness and/or access to capital.	Comply or explain principle mandated by the regulator since 2001; disclosure to the public; improve shareholders' participation, information and voting; institutional investors disclosure of voting policies; restrictions to anti-takeover defences; at least one independent director.
Slovak Republic	None.		

CORPORATE GOVERNANCE: A SURVEY OF OECD COUNTRIES – ISBN 92-64-10605-7 – © OECD 2004

Table 2.2. **Summary of codes and principles in operation
and their predecessors** (cont.)

Excluding specific principles such as those of investment funds

Nation	Code	Main objectives	Instruments
Spain	Olivencia Report (February 1998).	Improve companies' performance, competitiveness and/or access to capital.	Board's mission to create "shareholder value"; "broad majority" of non-executive directors, within whom independent directors in proportion to the floating capital; same proportion within executive committees; counterbalances within the board to CEO-Chair; establish other kinds of committees; remuneration tied to company's results; limits and controls to related-party transactions; improve shareholders' participation, information and voting.
	Informe de la Comisión Especial para el Fomento de la Transparancia y Seguridad en los Mercados y en las Sociedades Coti, January 2003.		Confirm Olivencia Report; suggestion to Government and Parliament to enact legislation to have listed enterprises: *i)* adopt the comply-or-explain principle; *ii)* define in a more detailed way the conflicts of interest of directors; *iii)* adopt a CG code.
Sweden	Swedish Shareholders Association Policy (November 1999 and October 2001).	Improve accountability to shareholders and/or maximise shareholder value.	Improve shareholders' participation, information and voting; important that institutional investors exercise their influence; decisions on the company's capital (share issues, buyback/reselling) should not be delegated to the board; the board should comprise only non-executives, except the managing director; separation CEO-Chair; establish nomination, audit and remuneration committees nominated by shareholders entirely made up of non-executive directors where minority shareholders will be represented; stock option plans conditioned on transparency and quantitative limits.
Switzerland	Swiss code of best practice for corporate governance (Swiss Code), Swiss Business Federation, July 2002.	Improve transparency including group structure and compensation, improve work of the board, tighten shareholder rights.	Voluntary. One-share-one-vote principle not contained in the code; improve shareholders' participation, information and voting; board made up of a majority of non-executive directors; in case of CEO-Chair, counterbalances within the board; establish audit and remuneration committees made of a majority of non-executive directors; compensation proportional to company's results and individual contribution.
	Corporate governance Directive, SWX Swiss Exchange, April 2002.	Encourage issuers to transparency.	Combination of mandatory and comply or explain principles; transparency of significant (group of) shareholders, capital structure, board composition, compensation and loans to board members, voting-rights restrictions.
Turkey	Under preparation.		

Table 2.2. **Summary of codes and principles in operation
and their predecessors** (cont.)

Excluding specific principles such as those of investment funds

Nation	Code	Main objectives	Instruments
United Kingdom	Higgs Report January 2003.	Review of the role and effectiveness of non-executive directors through proposed revisions to the Combined Code.	Now included in Combined Code. Improve quality and accountability of independent directors; strengthened oversight of audit and accountancy; 1/2 independent non-executive directors within the board (chairman excluded); separation chair-CEO; nomination committee of a majority of independent directors headed by the chair; remuneration committee entirely of independent directors. Senior independent director to facilitate dialogue with investors.
	Combined Code (July 1998). Last update June 2003.	Improve quality of board (supervisory) governance; improve quality of governance-related information available to equity markets.	Principles embracing Cadbury, Greenbury and Hampel reports updated for Higgs and a report on audit committee. Comply or explain principle required by LSE listing rules; Comply section now to include main and supporting principles. From 2004 half directors to be independent outsiders but for small firms only 2 are required. Remuneration report now part of company law. Chairman to be independent. Self evaluation of board. Planned and progressive refreshing of the board. Board to maintain contacts with shareholders. Institutional shareholders should have contacts with company and have a responsibility to make considered use of their votes.
United States	Commission on Public Trust and Private Enterprise, Conference Board (Peterson Report), January 2003.	Address widespread abuses which led to recent corporate scandals and declining public trust in companies, their leaders and America's capital markets.	Voluntary. Principles established for audit and accounting; better balance between board and CEO functions; more independent directors and better qualified; ethics oversight; greater shareholder involvement; transparent compensation tied to company performance.
	Corporate governance rules proposals, NYSE, April 2003.	Review of NYSE listing standards.	Listing standard. Costing of stock options, increased board independence, stronger nomination, compensation and audit committees; shareholder approval of options plans.
	Corporate governance and listing standards, Nasdaq, March 2003	Review of Nasdaq listing standards.	Listing standard. Costing of stock options, increased board independence, stronger nomination, compensation and audit committees

CORPORATE GOVERNANCE: A SURVEY OF OECD COUNTRIES – ISBN 92-64-10605-7 – © OECD 2004

Table 2.2. **Summary of codes and principles in operation
and their predecessors** (cont.)

Excluding specific principles such as those of investment funds

Nation	Code	Main objectives	Instruments
	Principles of corporate governance, Business Roundtable, May 2002 (also September 1997).	Advance the ability of US public corporations to compete, create jobs, and generate economic growth.	Voluntary. Directors' monitoring role of management on behalf of stockholders; establish committees; establish a code of conduct for management; a "substantial number" of independent directors within the board; establish committees, in particular nominating and compensation committee only of independent directors.
	Report of the NACD Blue Ribbon Commission on director Professionalism, 1996, reissued 2001.	Create and maintain an audit committee that adds value to the board and the corporation.	Voluntary. Audit committees should be established by boards regardless of company's size; the committee's performance should be evaluated against a charter; competent and independent directors should chair the committee.

1. Outside directors are defined as directors "capable of performing their duties independently from the management, controlling shareholders and the corporation".

Source: OECD, based on information provided by national authorities.

codes. However, in some cases such as in Germany "comply or explain" refers only to what are regarded as key elements. In a number of other countries, the code is administered by a stock market through its listing requirements but it is often not clear whether "comply or explain" is actually enforced or even monitored. Enforcement raises the question of sanctions but delisting, which is often implied, would appear to be a heavy handed instrument which could actually harm the investors the code is trying to protect. In some countries investors might seek to enforce codes by claiming that non-compliance leaves a board outside a "safe-harbour" with respect to interpreting the law. It is too early to tell whether this possibility might be abused by investors. Some countries such as Korea and Portugal have established formal follow-up reporting procedures by independent bodies. However, in a number of countries there is also uncertainty about whether the exercise could become one of box ticking and thus frustrate the original intention of the codes or principles. For example, in support of the Cromme Commission's Kodex, a new amendment to German corporate law calls for supervisory boards to assess their effectiveness each year against a set of criteria. Only time will tell whether the incentives are sufficient for the supervisory board to engage in a serious exercise in self-assessment or whether – in view of the fairly autonomous nature of the board with its limited accountability to clearly defined stakeholders (including shareholders) – it will become an exercise in box ticking.

University of Ulster
LIBRARY

What do we know about compliance with existing codes and principles?

Although voluntary codes and principles have the advantage of maintaining flexibility and avoiding excessive and costly legal and regulatory measures, the question of their effectiveness does arise. On the positive side, the pioneering Cadbury Report in the UK led to significant changes in board structure and management characteristics.[4] The recommendations of this report were adopted by the London Stock Exchange on a "comply or explain" basis, with verification by outside auditors. There was also a certain threat of legislative action in the report if companies did not comply with the guidelines. The Spanish authorities report around 80 per cent compliance with the full recommendations of the old (and perhaps not very ambitious) Olivencia Code and a follow-up report in Italy suggests quite high compliance and a marked improvement in board structure and in some areas of transparency, but excluding control arrangements.[5] Both the Mexican and German authorities report a compliance rate of approximately 70 per cent, with a tendency for compliance with board-related measures to rise.[6] On the other hand, although many codes and principles are too new to allow firm conclusions to be drawn, the recent track record in the UK, Netherlands, Canada, Portugal and Australia does raise some questions:

- According to a report by the shareholder activist group PIRC,[7] two thirds of British companies do not fully comply with the voluntary standards on corporate governance three years after the Combined Code was introduced. In particular, a number of companies still combine the roles of chief executive and chairman, which in the view of the UK code, blurs the line of accountability. Moreover, too few have sufficient numbers of independent directors (firms decide on the definition themselves making comparison difficult) and 75 per cent of boards remain controlled by directors who are not independent. The independence of remuneration and nomination committees remained questionable. The incentive structure facing external auditors had not greatly changed either, with the average FTSE company paying its external accountants twice as much in consulting as in audit fees.

- Only around one third of Canada's top 313 firms meet all corporate governance disclosure requirements set by the Toronto Stock Exchange's guidelines. Moreover, the quality of corporate governance disclosure, a stock exchange listing requirement, appears to be low for many companies.[8]

- In the Netherlands, despite a move by some large companies in 2002 to empower shareholders, a follow-up on implementation of the 40 voluntary recommendations of the 1997 Peters Committee found that boards continue to curb shareholder rights and that institutional investors have not been active enough to counter such practices.[9] Indeed, less than half of the listed companies complied with the Peters Committee recommendation that they "comply or explain". As a result, a new panel was set up, publishing a new code in December 2003 that recommends a legal obligation to "comply or explain".

- In Portugal, only 3 per cent of companies comply with the recommendation to encourage the exercise of voting rights and the figure for the provision of information for voting and to have one or more directors independent of the dominant stakeholder is 7 and 46 per cent respectively.[10]

- An Australian survey found that out of 250 listed companies some 30 per cent had governance structures deficient in terms of the standards set by the Australian Investment and Financial Services Association.[11] Nearly all had audit committees but less than one third had nomination committees. More importantly, only a third had audit and remuneration committees with a majority of independent members.

Low compliance may reflect the fact that the instruments are simply not appropriate for many firms but if very low it would also raise questions about the general applicability of the principles themselves. Two studies have examined lack of compliance in more detail. In the Netherlands the voluntary principles were intended, *inter alia*, to increase the role of shareholders.[12] With such a fundamental change, it is hardly surprising that one study found that the recommendations had no substantive effect on corporate governance characteristics despite the fact that empirical results suggest that corporate profitability in firms with more accountability to investors performed much better.[13] The situation is thus similar to the experience in Portugal where compliance with the voting principles has been poor. Clearly, the efficacy of self-regulation depends on who holds shareholder voting rights and the existence of an effective relationship between the capital markets and board decisions.[14] The situation in Canada is quite different. The 14 guidelines follow the Principles closely in defining the responsibilities of the board and in seeking to increase its effectiveness. Yet at least over a period of several years, the usual incentives to disclose more information voluntarily did not appear to apply to the quality of information about corporate governance.[15] Poor disclosure may also simply reflect the actual behaviour of companies.

Low compliance in Portugal also illustrates some of the dynamics and pitfalls involved. As in Australia, the more sophisticated sectors appear to comply quite well. The authorities have argued that overall low compliance reflects the dominance of large family shareholders and the state, which should reduce agency costs and improve governance. However, this would only be the case if protection of minority shareholders was assured.

The above experiences are still rather preliminary and might well change as markets become more sensitive to corporate governance arrangements as a factor determining longer run returns and the avoidance of crises. Good governance funds are still rather new and the average voting level by institutions is gradually changing: the voting level by institutions in the TSE All Share index is now 56 per cent, up from 51 per cent last year. In cases such as Portugal where the ownership structure serves to distance firms from market pressures, the situation will probably take longer to evolve in the absence of major shareholders adapting their own activity. Greater protection for minority shareholders would certainly spur such a rethink in these cases, aided perhaps by unorthodox policy measures such as the corporate governance black list now issued by the Portuguese authorities. But it is probably best to keep in mind that merely adopting recommended structures and practices is not the ultimate solution to ensuring good corporate governance. As an Australian Parliamentary report noted: "A cursory investigation of companies involved in recent corporate failures and fraud reveal that they may have exhibited the trappings of good corporate governance, such as an audit committee, a statement of corporate governance practices in the annual report, and the existence of non-executive directors on the board... Outward compliance with good corporate governance principles is not sufficient guarantee of their effective operation."[16]

Notes

1. Regulatory impact assessment methodology is well developed in Canada and has been used to document recent proposals concerning company law changes in the UK.

2. The German Panel on Corporate Governance (*Grundsatzkommission Corporate Governance*) raised these fundamental issues although, with one exception, it has not led, as yet, to changes in the nature of company law. They have also been raised in the Belgium parliament during debate around the Corporate Governance Act in 2002 and again in 2003 in the context of executive remuneration. For a fuller discussion see P. Hommelhoff, "The OECD Principles on Corporate Governance: Opportunities and Risks from the Perspective of the German Corporate Governance Movement", *International and Comparative Corporate Law Journal*, Vol. 2, 2001.

3. For a more detailed assessment confined to EU countries see *Comparative study of corporate governance codes relevant to the European Union and its Member States*, Weil, Gotshal and Manges, Brussels, 2002.

4. J. Dahya, J. McConnell and N. Travlos, "The Cadbury Committee: corporate performance and management turnover", *Journal of Finance*, 2001.

5. *Analisi dello stato di attuazione del Codice di Autodisciplina delle societa quotate (Anno 2002)*, Assonime, Rome, February 2003.

6. For Germany, a study commissioned by the government of 99 large public companies (DAX and MDAX) showed a very high rate of compliance of around 90 per cent with the Kodex (*i.e.* 90 per cent of the 30 enterprises in the DAX have brought 59 of 62 recommendations into force). However, the survey relates to the core elements of the Kodex and not to more aspirational recommendations (*i.e. sollte, kann*). See *Umsetzung des Deutschen Corporate Governance Kodex in Börsennotierten Gesellschaften*, Berlin 19 May 2003. See *www.bccg.tu-berlin.de*.

7. PIRC's *Annual Review of Corporate Governance*, December 2002, see *www.pirc.co.uk*.

8. B. McConony and M. Bujaki, "Corporate governance: factors influencing voluntary disclosure by publicly traded Canadian firms", *Canadian Accounting Perspectives*, No. 2, Fall 2002. See also R. Labelle, *The Statement of Corporate Governance Practices: a Voluntary Disclosure and Corporate Governance Perspective*, mimeo, HEC Montreal, June 2002.

9. The follow-up study is "Corporate governance 2002, de stand van zaken", *Nederlandse Corporate Governance Stichting*, 2002. More recent developments covering the large firms are reported in *Trends and Results*, Deminor, April 2003.

10. Portuguese Securities Commission (CMVM), *4th Survey on Corporate Governance Practices*, Lisbon, 2002.

11. *Horwath 2002 Corporate Governance Report*, Horwath Sydney 2002. Some of the companies with low corporate governance scores were also quite large and successful.

12. Supervisory boards of large Dutch companies working under the "structural regime" are not elected by shareholders and new board members are simply "co-opted". Moreover, a number of firms have used a system by which shares are held by a depository that issues receipts without voting rights to investors. As a result, takeover defences are also strong. For details see Abe de Jong, *et al.*, "Ownership and control in the Netherlands", in F. Barca and M. Becht eds, *The Control of Corporate Europe*, Oxford, 2001. As noted in the text, there is now an agreement to change the "structural regime" so that members of the supervisory board will be appointed by the meeting of shareholders.

13. D. DeJong *et al.*, *The role of self regulation in corporate Governance: evidence from the Netherlands*, mimeo, University of Iowa, October 2001.

14. The findings also point to the difficulty of using self-regulation to deal with the fundamental issue of balance of power in a corporation. The latter would normally be a political decision although the full economic consequences may not be adequately taken into account.

15. In particular, the study found no consistent and significant relationship between the disclosure quality of corporate governance and firm performance or other corporate governance variables such as the structure of the board and the level of financing activity.

16. Paragraph 2.8, *Review of Independent Auditing by Registered Company Auditors*, Joint Committee of Public Accounts, House of Representatives, Canberra, 2000.

ISBN 92-64-10605-7
Corporate Governance: A Survey of OECD Countries
© OECD 2004

Chapter 3

Thematic Review of Developments and Emerging Issues

Voluntary principles and changes to corporate law and regulation have focused, in the first instance, on questions to do with board composition and duties (including controlling conflicts of interest) in the judgement that this is the key institution where problems have arisen. In many ways it has also been an area where initiatives have been easiest to agree. The second most important area has been in disclosure and in particular with respect to the functions of external auditors. On the other hand, fundamental questions such as the exercise of ownership rights and other corporate governance issues, such as the role of stakeholders, have been the subject of less activity. This chapter follows the order set out in the Principles and each section highlights the connection with the relevant passages and the interrelationship between them.

The rights of shareholders and their equitable treatment

At the heart of any governance system is the concept of the shareholder, the delegation of responsibility for managing the usual affairs of the enterprise to another group, and the set of rights which preserves the value to shareholders of this delegation. The relevant sections of the Principles state that the "*corporate governance framework should protect shareholders rights, which includes equitable treatment for all shareholders including minority and foreign shareholders*". Moreover, "*all shareholders should have the opportunity to obtain effective redress for violation of their rights*". More specifically:

- Principle I.D "*Capital structure and arrangements that enable certain shareholders to obtain a degree of control disproportionate to their equity ownership should be disclosed*";

- Principle I.E "*markets for corporate control should be allowed to function in an efficient and transparent manner*";

- Principle I.E.2 "*Anti-take-over devices should not be used to shield management from accountability*";

- Principle I.F "*Shareholders, including institutional investors, should consider the costs and benefits of exercising their voting rights*";

- Principle II.A.2, "*Votes should be cast by custodians of nominees in a manner agreed upon with the beneficial owners of the shares*";

- Principle II.B "*Insider trading and abusive self-dealing should be prohibited*"; and,

- Principle II.C "*Members of the board and managers should be required to disclose any material interests in transactions or matters affecting the corporation*".

Recent experience has underlined the essential importance of the Principles, while pointing to a number of additional issues which need to be dealt with if shareholders are to be able to exercise their control rights effectively. The key issues which stand out include: i) improving the possibilities for shareholder voice to be effective including via strengthened voting rights; ii) greater disclosure by some institutional investors of their voting policies; iii) tightening control of the board including better enforcement of the liability of directors and auditors; and iv) facilitating the contestability of corporate control while protecting the rights of minority shareholders. The latter has been shown to be important in the presence of large shareholders, with important consequences for growth and equity.

Improving shareholder voice and enforcing rights

Although a superficial review of the OECD's company law and corporate governance data base shows that shareholders have the power to elect board members of their choice in most countries, and thereby to demand accountability by the board and ultimately management, the reality is often quite different. In some countries such as the Netherlands, board members in a number of companies are essentially appointed by the existing board (i.e. co-opted). In other countries, it is formally shareholders who elect board members. However, crucial to what actually happens is who has the power to nominate and to set the list of nominees when by law or through a company's by-laws, the list might be all the shareholders get to vote on to either accept or reject. In some cases, it is only the proposal by the board and thereby often incumbent management that is available for shareholders to ratify and it is not possible to vote against a particular candidate.[1] Staggered boards whereby, for example, with a three year term only one third of the members are standing for election each year is another device which dilutes shareholder power. Proxy contests are in any case expensive and with firms able to use all the resources they need to ensure that their list is accepted, the corporate election process is, as a practical matter, rendered an irrelevancy.[2] To alleviate the problem some countries (e.g. United States, United Kingdom) have now established nomination committees comprising independent board members (see below). But as two judges note, "... there will remain the danger that incumbent slates will remain overly comfortable in their positions and that even putatively independent directors will become less than ideally sensitive to stockholder input".[3] Such considerations have led to a more structural response beginning to take shape in some countries. Korea, for example, has introduced cumulative voting as a possibility, which would allow minority shareholders to concentrate support on particular candidates, although few firms are opting for this option. In the United States, the SEC issued a public call on May 1st requesting suggestions on how to improve regulations covering corporate director elections as part of its review of their proxy rules. The Commission proposed rules to increase proxy access by shareholders subject to certain conditions on 8th October 2003 and a decision is expected in the first half of 2004.[4]

The ability of shareholders to table proposals and to ask questions of directors (*i.e.* to demand accountability) appears to be, in reality, very limited in a number of countries and especially so in Italy and Spain.[5] More importantly, in a number of cases the vote is strictly advisory and binds the board in no way. This situation begs the question of why vote. As noted by Bebchuk, the formal limitations of management/director power do not correspond to the common law/ civil law distinction.[6] Thus, the power of shareholders in the US to overturn board decisions and to question directors is very limited but this is not the case in the UK, Australia, New Zealand and Canada. In the UK, for example, shareholders have a common law right to propose resolutions at an annual shareholder meeting.[7] They are only required to give notice to shareholders and to bear the cost of the notice. Shareholder proposals in the US are first lodged with the firm. If the firm refuses to include the proposal in their proxy statements, the company must request a no-action letter from the SEC which reviews all excluded proposals.[8] This procedure is now subject to a thorough review by the SEC.

Adequate disclosure is key to the effective use by shareholders of their rights and the Principles advocate that it include details of payments to board members and key executives. Such information is crucial for shareholders to judge the competence and independence of board members. But beyond that there is the question of whether shareholders should be given more decision rights with respect to board and key executive compensation in order to deal with conflicts of interest by board members. This is currently a controversial issue in Sweden with proposals that shareholders should approve the remuneration package. In general, total board compensation is approved by the meeting of shareholders in Japan although in companies moving to the single board system, compensation appears to be determined by the compensation committee without approval by the annual general meeting. Shareholders now vote on directors' remuneration in the UK (but not for executives as such where there is not considered to be a conflict of interest) though the vote is not for approval but of an advisory nature.[9] Some observers criticise this as a hybrid, which is bound to create difficulties. Nevertheless, it has been effective recently in rolling back some board compensation decisions when it became clear to the companies involved that they risked losing the advisory vote. More generally, there is a good case for shareholder approval, especially if the power to replace board members is effectively limited. However, approval should be restricted to setting the policy guidelines and not the individual employment contracts and payment claims of board members and executives where discretion is important in dynamic markets. The recent Expert Group on European Corporate Law has recommended this latter route.[10] Nevertheless, the experience in the US, where shareholders' approval of options packages has often been general in the extreme, and probably ineffective, needs to be kept in mind.[11] In June 2003, the SEC approved new rules that were adopted by the NYSE and Nasdaq, which require shareholder approval of equity compensation plans as well as any material revisions to such plans.

Another area where there might be a need for more shareholder decision making concerns the frustration of take-over bids by the board of a target company. The issue is less one about the structure of the company's control such as voting caps and multiple voting shares that would normally be established by the respective articles of the company – and which should be disclosed – but their introduction as part of a take-over defence. In this area there is a wide difference between jurisdictions especially in the EU. Golden shares in some privatised enterprises can also give EU governments a very wide range of discretion.

A crucial area concerns disclosure of shareholding structures, including pyramids, which result in control rights being greater than cash flow rights. Despite a number of initiatives such as scrutiny of voting agreements by the competition authority in Italy, information appears to be scarce. With greater concern to identify beneficial owners due to issues related to crime and tax evasion, it might be an appropriate time to reinforce disclosure from a governance perspective.[12] Shareholder identity is an issue in several countries. Canadian companies are under no obligation since July 2002 to send proxy materials to shareholders who do not disclose their underlying identity and new French regulations go so far as to hand boards the power to strip voting and dividend rights of anonymous investors.

More stringent requirements for disclosure even within the context of codes and principles might require improved enforcement of shareholder rights beyond that which market sanctions would bring: disclosure might after all not be complete or truthful. In the US there is resort to derivative and class action law suits. Within the EU, there is a special investigation procedure in Germany, France, the UK, Netherlands, Belgium, and Denmark, and outside the EU in Switzerland. The instrument is potentially of considerable importance for minority shareholders although in some countries there have been only a few cases. A successful special investigation can serve the basis of a court claim, and in some instances the two are closely linked. At stake here is the liability of board members (and auditors) but one which does not compromise the important business judgement rule. Penalties could include disqualification to act as a director and forfeiture of bonuses, etc. There is unease in some countries (*e.g.* Australia) that, unless carefully defined, personal liability of directors might act as a disincentive to becoming a director and could serve to reduce entrepreneurial but responsible risk taking activity. For the United States one study shows that the possibility to hold outside directors personally liable has been quite remote, at least up till the recent strengthening in enforcement.[13]

The reason for the widely varying use of enforcement mechanisms appears to be differences in the standing of individual and minority shareholders and other procedural law rules.[14] Some civil law countries, including Sweden and Germany, are looking at the matter again to see if Canadian and US experience could lead to reforms. Germany has promised reforms for 2004-2005 including the introduction of class action law suits. Korea is in the process of introducing such suits, albeit limited to window dressing, false information and insider trading. Nevertheless, as Hopt observes, the actual practice in Europe of penalising directors and improving the potential for bringing action against directors and auditors is likely to vary widely. Countries may approach the issue quite differently, "be it through a derivative action of each shareholder or a small majority of shareholders, opening the possibility for bundling shareholder actions, introducing a kind of company and capital market class action or, last but not least, by giving the courts or a supervisory office the right to disqualify a person from serving as a director of companies (across the EU) and to initiate restitution proceedings against a director".[15] In the US, the Sarbanes Oxley Act has strengthened civil and criminal enforcement and has given the SEC additional authority to bar individuals from serving as officers and directors of public companies. Moreover, the SEC was required to study its past enforcement actions and to identify areas where these proceedings may be used to provide effective restitution for injured investors. It is also charged with reviewing other methods of providing restitution to injured investors that may be more efficient and effective, and to report its findings to Congress.

Ensuring the integrity of financial service providers

In exercising their ownership rights, shareholders have to rely on agents such as brokers, investment advisors, analysts, research and rating agencies for information, and in this area recent experience points to a number of issues. The matter of competence is best left to the market to control but inappropriate incentives and conflicts of interest appear to represent a more serious problem. For example, analysts working for investment banks have been under pressure to give favourable recommendations about firms with which the bank has a commercial relationship, including lucrative initial public offerings. Ratings companies, which are paid by a company to produce a rating, might also be subject to a conflict of interests with a resulting bias to produce a better rating.

In cases where there is a contractual relation between the investor and the agent there is a legal if not very economic remedy, but for others such as analysts and rating agencies this is far from clear. More concrete rules about professional duties of analysts and how to handle conflicts of interest may be necessary and could take the form of either stock exchange rules or professional codes of conduct.[16] This course of action is being taken in some countries. Full disclosure of potential conflicts of interest is also important since it may amplify reputation effects in the market. Other potential solutions are more structural and go to the heart of the structure of incentives. Among the measures being proposed are firewalls to separate bonuses for analysts from the wider profits of the company. Time will tell how effective they are especially when stock and bond markets recover and incentives to present optimistic buy recommendations increase once again.

Improving and facilitating the exercise of voting rights

The exercise of voting rights appears to vary widely between countries: a recent study by Institutional Analysis, the University of Melbourne and Corporate Governance International showed that investors cast only 33 per cent of total votes in Australia in 2000 compared with 83 per cent in the US, 71-80 per cent in Japan and 50 per cent in the UK. The reasons for this difference in participation vary. For example, the high level in Japan reflects the need to meet a quorum requirement, and with most annual shareholder meetings occurring on the same day, management is careful to muster all the proxy votes from its friendly shareholders.[17] There is also a quorum requirement in the US which gives an incentive for firms to identify and send proxy material to their shareholders; listed companies in the US are required to send proxies at their own expense to all shareholders whether in street name or not.

In Australia and the EU efforts are underway to raise ballot turnout through, for example, better use of electronic communications. But it is also necessary to lower the costs and to improve the facilities, particularly for cross-border voting. A high level report for the EU into cross-border voting, which is important due to international shareholdings by institutions and private investors, noted that shareholder meetings requiring physical presence no longer offer a sufficient central forum for shareholder information, communication, and decision making. The report identified legal and practical problems to cross-border voting within the EU arising from: i) the identification of shareholders entitled to vote in situations where shares are held through chains of intermediaries across borders; ii) current formalities for the exercise of voting rights; iii) differences in settlement times of share transfers across borders; and, iv) the practice of stock lending. The problem of cross border voting is, however, widespread in the OECD area. One study followed actual transactions between five issuers (in the US, UK, Germany, Japan and Italy) and six investment managers from both the US and the UK. The study found that investment managers found it difficult in some countries to verify whether their global custodians/voting agents had received and acted upon their voting instructions, and even where they could verify this they were rarely able to audit the onward transmission of these instructions to sub-custodians and company registrars.[18] Many of the problems need to be addressed by legal changes and regulatory changes which might need to involve increasing the minimum notice period for firms to better correspond to the needs of foreign investors. In some jurisdictions it is already possible for notice periods to be increased but companies choose to retain the minimum period. This is an area the OECD might need to examine more thoroughly in support of efficient capital movements.

As illustrated in Table 1.1.B and documented more fully elsewhere, institutional investors have become major shareholders in the OECD area so that their role in corporate governance has become an issue in many countries. The EU Action Plan calls for them to disclose their voting policies, and regulations to this effect have been tightened in the US. The rights and duties of institutional shareholders is a major policy issue in the UK, and in Australia and France[19] the issue has come to the forefront, in the former following a committee of enquiry. In Japan, the association of pension funds has introduced a code of conduct, calling for a more active voting policy.[20] The issues are complex involving as they do potential conflicts of interest and disclosure, the cost benefit calculation of taking a more active voting policy, and the danger of codes, laws etc becoming too prescriptive. At a minimum, it would seem necessary to distinguish between those institutional investors acting in a fiduciary capacity from more general institutions which nevertheless still provide important services by creating liquidity and by underpinning the formation of equity prices.

Although there are investment funds and institutional investors for which the exercise of voting rights is not important (i.e. they vote with their feet), in other cases concerning those institutions acting in a fiduciary capacity it might be of concern for investors to know if and how the fund has exercised its voting rights. It is also argued that such information is important for investors, so they can know whether there is a conflict of interest when the management is also seeking business from the firm in which it holds shares. The counter argument is the expense of maintaining such information and that disclosure could lead to political pressures to support certain firms. However, the former objection would seem surmountable if there is no question of funds voting according to the wishes of individual investors. The SEC has taken this view and in February 2003 ruled that US mutual funds (with around 100 million investors and $6.5 trillion in assets) must disclose ballot decisions annually by no later than August 2004 (for the 12 month period beginning July 1st 2003 and ending 30th June 2004). The relevant regulator is also considering whether the ruling should also apply to bank trusts which control at least 5 per cent of proxy votes at US firms. More importantly, they also hold their own shares in trust which strengthens the control of the board.[21]

The development of large institutional investors could, nevertheless, strengthen corporate governance since these funds have both an interest and the capability to monitor company performance, and not inconsiderable power to do something about it. However, it appears to matter very much how the institutional investors are organised and their own governance arrangements. One study of public and private pension funds in the US shows that only in the case of private funds is there a shared interest with other shareholders and this is associated with better firm performance once all channels of influence with the firm are taken into account.[22] This result appears to be due to clear fiduciary responsibility and performance-based pay of the funds. Public funds in the study were not subject to the same tight fiduciary duty and many faced no tight budget restriction in so far as the taxpayer will step in to bail them out if they cannot meet their defined benefit plans. With many fund heads elected, it is not surprising that the agenda of the funds is different and this is also reflected in a weak incentive structure for managers. Such funds have been, nevertheless, very active in putting forward shareholder proposals, but these do not appear to have been very effective.[23] More importantly, even if effective it is not clear that such funds have the same interests as other shareholders.

The level of disclosure sought by various national bodies and principles from institutional investors can be quite extensive and include the level of resources devoted to monitoring. The latter is driven by a number of observers who feel that despite grand statements, the corporate governance expert on an investment team remains a junior partner and the publicised change in policy direction superficial. For example, in referring to pension funds, one set of recommended national principles states that "managers should have an explicit strategy including the circumstances in which it will intervene in a company; the approach they will use in doing so; and how they measure the effectiveness of this strategy". It also calls for a statement of investment principles to be issued. Other approaches have been developed by investor groups such as the Institutional Shareholders Committee that calls for institutions and their agents to: "set out their policy on how they will discharge their responsibilities, clarifying the priorities attached to particular issues and when they will take action; monitor the performance of, and establish, where necessary, a regular dialogue with companies; intervene where necessary; evaluate the impact of their activism; and report back to clients/beneficial shareholders."

In response to widespread concern to protect private pension schemes by improving their governance, the OECD established *Guidelines for Pension Fund Governance* in 2002. The 12 point guidelines include specific proposals for:

- The appropriate legal and governance structures to ensure funds are managed in the best interest of plan members and beneficiaries.
- The accountability, integrity and professionalism of individuals on funds' governing bodies.
- Transparency and rules for communication between fund managers and plan members.
- Actuarial certification, independent auditing and the role of both actuaries and auditors as "whistleblowers".

Changes in control and equitable treatment

One of the most contentious issues in the OECD area concerns the market for corporate control and the degree to which control is contestable. Control changes more often than is recognised in a number of countries but this has not prevented attention focussing on takeovers and especially hostile ones, which are practically unknown in a number of countries. Concentrated share ownership is one reason for this situation but there are also formal and informal barriers in most countries. One reason for formal barriers is that a number of governments remain sceptical about the benefits of hostile take-overs and can be strongly influenced by a powerful combination of entrenched management and employees to the neglect of other stakeholders and longer run considerations.[24] However, there is a cost to the policy. Although takeovers may not always lead to improved performance by the new group, takeovers and the threat of them may at least put a floor under board performance and limit the costs when other corporate governance mechanisms have proved ineffective. The policy shields management from accountability and prevents markets for corporate control from functioning in an efficient and transparent manner, two key elements of the Principles. Greater management entrenchment is in turn often associated with poorer performance by the companies involved (Box 1.3).

In assessing the contestability of corporate control it is necessary to look at the governance system as a whole rather than focus on specific measures and instruments which can be misleading. For example, enterprises in the US are allowed to take defensive measures even after a bid has been made and poison pill defences are widespread. By contrast, in the UK post-bid defences are not permitted unless approved by shareholders and in Germany poison pills arrangements are not possible due to the strong pre-emption rights of existing shareholders. To form conclusions about the contestability and efficiency of the market for control and the accountability of board members and management, a broader perspective is necessary. Thus, in the US, poison pills and takeover defences must be seen in the light of bargaining about the price being offered. Empirical studies point to take-over defences being a particular problem when the board is dominated by insiders (and therefore serving to entrench management) but it is less of an issue when the board is more outsider oriented and also motivated in part through shareholdings (Box 1.3). The lack of defences in the UK, which is demanded by institutional investors, is accompanied by a bidding system which has the effect of raising the price.[25] On the other hand, the lack of poison pills, voting caps and multiple voting shares in Germany does not mean that there is a contestable market for corporate control. The multi-year, overlapping term, of supervisory board members makes it difficult for anyone to obtain control, in addition to the structure of shareholdings, particularly those held in custody by banks which unless expressly instructed can exercise the voting rights as they please, in practice in favour of existing management.

Recent developments since the Principles were agreed illustrate how difficult it is to establish a contestable and efficient market for corporate control, since there is an inbuilt weakness in negotiating a level playing field when institutional differences make that difficult to define, and where bargaining strategy is also important. The EU's 13th Directive concerning takeovers promised progress but was defeated in the EU parliament over concerns that a level playing field was not being achieved. Germany subsequently passed a new takeover law which gave the supervisory board power, following approval by shareholders that is valid for 18 months, to approve defensive measures taken by the management board, although what the latter can actually do is unclear. The issues concern the lack of defensive instruments which are available in some other countries such as golden shares. In Europe, as in the United States, barriers to takeovers differ widely across jurisdictions. In EU countries such as Sweden and France, dual shareholding structures involving multiple or double voting rights are frequent, and in the Netherlands shares are often held by a depository which do not generally have fiduciary responsibilities with respect to voting the shares in custody.[26] In some other countries such structures are not permitted but there are other provisions such as consent for the transfer of shares, voting caps and limits to the rights to appoint or dismiss board members. The latter may be a particularly pernicious barrier to takeovers leading the European Experts Group on Company Law to propose a break-through rule for the bidder if it has obtained a sufficient number of shares to enable the statutes of the company to be modified. In Switzerland and in the Netherlands a number of large enterprises have now voluntarily given up defences such as voting caps and depository certificates to improve their standing in the world capital markets and to lower their cost of capital.

A key issue in thinking about the market for corporate control is the equitable treatment of all shareholders, including an equitable distribution of the control premium being offered by a bidder. However, there might be a trade-off between equitable treatment and facilitating contestability of control. In order to protect shareholders, the UK, most of the other EU countries and Australia have mandatory bid rules. Such rules do not exist in the US although in practice it seems as if bidders end up making an offer to all shareholders. In Australia, a mandatory bid is required when a bidder reaches 25 per cent ownership, a level regarded as so low that it could serve as a takeover deterrent. In other countries it is usually much higher. For example, Spain has now amended its take-over code to protect shareholders requiring bidders to launch a full takeover within two years once they have acquired 50 per cent of the shares or control of its board. Before it was 75 per cent and did not include a time frame. The rationale for the bid rule is that it gives an early exit option for shareholders who fear ending up with a majority shareholder having control and exercising it to their detriment in the future. However, in practice it does not greatly help minority shareholders when the bidder has effective control of the company leading the Experts Group for the Reform of European Company law to propose a sell-out rule for minorities which would not pre-suppose a preceding takeover.

Protecting minority shareholders

An important issue touched upon in Chapter I but not expressly covered in the Principles is the rights of minority shareholders. The issue most clearly surfaces in OECD countries in the context of groups of companies, an issue not addressed directly in the Principles. In Italy, France, Belgium, Japan, Korea and the Czech Republic among others, the interests of minority shareholders could conflict with those of large shareholders, management and other stakeholders when a controlling company shifts assets away from the dominated company by *inter alia*, loan guarantees, transfer pricing, and by capital increases to which the subsidiary must subscribe. Such actions have been often judged to be legal as long as managers can justify their non-loyalty toward the subsidiary's minority shareholders by an overriding interest of the group of companies (duty of care) for which the standards of proof are not demanding. In France, Belgium and Italy, the judicial system has tended to give highest weight to the duty of care at the expense of the rival principle, the duty of loyalty, leading minority shareholders to lose lawsuits since their losses are not even considered.

Other legal and economic systems handle the problem in an entirely different manner. Common law countries tend to emphasise fairness when examining situations which have not been foreseen or categorised. In the case of fiduciary duty, "… the very fact that the interests of a director are in conflict with those of the company itself constitutes the basis for liability, and if the interests of the company are prejudiced as a result of such conflict, liability for breach of fiduciary duty arises".[27] In Germany, where stakeholders' interests are well defined, the issue is handled by an explicit law on groups of companies. Given the very strict separation of powers between the management and the supervisory board, even a shareholder with 70 per cent of the shares can have difficulty controlling a company. However, one company may enter into an agreement with the management board of another giving it full and unrestricted control, effectively disenfranchising the shareholders. In compensation, these shareholders have the right to either a dividend guarantee or a cash-out. Under this law of groups many cases of minority oppression are brought before the courts. However, the protective device is only *ex post* and has led to long judicial controversies, some of which have taken ten years to resolve. In contrast to shareholder protection, the German law lays down strict conditions for protecting creditors of the subsidiary.

The countries involved are well aware of the problem with company groups and the consequences, and in Belgium and Italy there have been initiatives to improve the situation. Lack of protection for minorities in group firms has stimulated the development of pyramids for corporate control and might explain the marked premium for controlling shares observed in a number of these countries.[28] As noted in Box 1.3, lack of protection of minority holders is associated with reduced performance. As a result, there has been some policy action in this area. The new Belgian law on corporate governance subjects significant operations involving a possible conflict of interest between members of a group of companies to specific procedures. To the extent that the interests of the dominated company and the potential harm to it are made transparent, there is a clear improvement over the status quo. However, shifting assets does not necessarily involve significant operations but often simply day to day pricing and marketing decisions. The new Italian corporate law also deals with pyramids in the context of group law. Directors of a subsidiary must adequately justify any decision that is affected by the influence of the controlling company and mention any such inter-group relations in their financial reporting. The law provides that shareholders and creditors may sue the controlling company for losses due to its "guidance" unless they are offset by gains that the subsidiary receives from being part of the group. Shareholders also have *ex ante* protection in that they may withdraw whenever their company enters or exits a group.[29] The EU's corporate governance action plan[30] also places high on the agenda the need to deal with pyramids and group companies. However, recourse by shareholders to legal remedies is still hindered by the length and cost of judicial procedures. Finally, concern that inadequate protection has real consequences in the presence of dominant shareholders led the Neue Markt in Germany and the Nouveau Marché in France to offer greater protection to minority shareholders.

Stakeholders

Stakeholders (such as creditors and employees) play an important role in a number of countries in influencing how corporate governance systems work in practice. Their interests are often protected by special legislation. Stakeholders are also active participants in determining the performance of a company and in monitoring the operation of the corporate governance system. These dual roles are recognised in the Principles. The relevant sections of the Principles state that the governance arrangements should *"encourage active co-operation between corporations and stakeholders in creating wealth, jobs and the sustainability of financially sound enterprises"*. Apart from the need for the company to meet the requirements of the law, Principle III.C of the Principles states that *"the corporate governance framework should permit performance enhancing mechanisms for stakeholder participation"*, and III.D recommends that *"where stakeholders participate in the corporate governance process, they should have access to relevant information"*. The chapter on disclosure (IV.A.6) also calls for information on *"material issues regarding employees and other stakeholders"* to be disclosed and developments in this area are taken up in the next section.

With respect to stakeholders as a concept, most agree that an essential component is the degree to which capital (human and physical) and other rights are tied to a given enterprise and therefore subject to possible losses from the action of, *inter alia*, management. Creditor rights are important in influencing both the access and terms of finance for companies, and typically arise from bankruptcy and other laws and the contractual relations established under them. Empirical work points towards the importance of established creditors rights for overall economic performance. Employee rights may derive as much from collective agreements or from international undertakings by a government (for example, with respect to the ILO) as from legal provisions. Performance enhancing mechanisms range from explicit economic incentives such as share distributions and forms of performance-related pay to the establishment of a corporate culture to motivate employees, employee consultation and representation on the boards. The mechanisms, and one possibly important for creditors, could also include undertakings about corporate disclosure by which the firm voluntarily commits to tighter standards than those required by applicable law. Although the different features of creditor and employee rights are well documented in the literature, analytical and empirical work on the effects of adhering to stakeholder principles is less well developed than in other areas of corporate governance, in part because of the difficulties of agreeing inclusive and standardised indicators.[31]

With respect to creditors, there are questions in some countries about contract enforcement and about how well the bankruptcy and insolvency systems are working, including the balance between reorganisation and liquidation.[32] Korea is in the process of reforming its bankruptcy system and is now moving to consolidate the various branches. Germany, Japan, and Italy have all been involved in reforming their systems in recent years and in some others, reviews are continuing. Bad debt resolution in the context of banking sector problems has underpinned the policy importance of the issue in Japan, Mexico and Korea. In a number of OECD countries, informal bank workouts or other arrangements appear to be important as indicated by the marked differences in the incidence of bankruptcy.[33] In some cases, such work-outs are an important complement to bankruptcy law allowing more flexible market instruments to operate. However, in some countries such as France and Italy, bankruptcy law hinders the process. The high incidence of work-outs in some countries may also reflect poor bankruptcy law and judicial delays. In these cases, work-outs may also be characterised by lack of transparency and can create moral hazards. Such concerns were in part responsible for the introduction of guidelines for work-outs (along the lines of the INSOL code) in Japan, although it has not been widely applied. From the viewpoint of understanding corporate governance systems for the development of policy, it is notable how little is actually known about creditor rights in a comparative context. This is because bankruptcy systems and enforcement are complex so that focusing on just some aspects through aggregate indicators, as early work did, may have created a false impression about relative performance.[34] While more is known about the incentive structures of various bankruptcy systems, much less is known about informal bank work-outs.

Customers and suppliers are sometimes identified as stakeholders if they may make costly and specific commitments to the company and are closely involved in contributing to its success. However, their interests are usually handled outside of the framework of corporate governance via private contractual arrangements and other market mechanisms. With respect to suppliers, it has been shown by empirical work associated with transactions costs theory that private contracts and financing evolve in all economies to deal with specific investments for a customer.[35] And a similar situation can occur between a customer and a supplier. Moreover, where contracts are incomplete since the exact state of the economy cannot be determined in advance, private institutions such as conciliation, both formal and informal, have evolved to fill the need for re-contracting. In short, in all advanced market economies relational transactions are more the norm than the exception but at the end of the day arrangements will depend not only on trust but also on efficient methods of contract enforcement including a framework for conciliation and arbitration. Even in the OECD region such pre-conditions are highly variable. The OECD *Guidelines for Multinational Enterprises* – an OECD voluntary code of conduct setting forth government-backed recommendations for multi-national enterprises – provides standards and principles for dealing with, *inter alia*, the complex stakeholder issues that emerge within the supply chain.

The issues surrounding employees as a stakeholder are even more difficult to examine from the corporate governance perspective, in part because of the complexity of such arrangements. Table 3.1.A indicates that while only seven countries require representatives of employees on the board, some seventeen have statutory provisions covering works councils, not including EU provisions covering European-wide companies. Such councils vary greatly in their powers to obtain information and in the nature of their role in decision making (Table 3.1.B). In some countries, it is a matter of

Table 3.1.A. **Some forms of employee participation in OECD countries**

	Employees appoint some board members	Works councils mandated by law	Constitutional reference to employee participation in the management of the company
Australia	No	No	No
Austria	Yes	Yes	No
Belgium	No	Yes	No
Canada	No	No	No
Czech Republic	Yes	No	No
Denmark	Yes	Yes	No
Finland	No	Yes	No
France	No	Yes	Constitutional right
Germany	Yes	Yes	No
Greece	No	Yes	No
Hungary	No	Yes	No
Ireland	No	No	No
Italy	No	No	Constitutional right
Japan	No	No	No
Korea	No	Yes	No
Mexico	No	No	No
Netherlands	No[1]	Yes	No
New Zealand	No	No	No
Norway	Yes	No	Constitutional right
Poland	No[2]	No[2]	No
Portugal	No	Yes	No
Slovak Republic	No	No	No
Spain	No	Yes	No
Sweden	Yes	No	No
Switzerland	No	No	No
Turkey	No	No	No
United Kingdom	No	No	No
United States	No	No	No

1. In the Netherlands the works council will be able to nominate a third of the Supervisory Board if a new law passes the upper house of parliament.
2. Employees have a right to appoint board members in companies with a State Treasury shareholding. A works council is mandated for state-owned enterprises.

Source: Based on Lopez-de-Silanes *et al.* 2003 and corrections by the OECD.

Table 3.1.B. **The coverage of mandated works councils**

	Statutory threshold	Information entitlement	Consultation issues	Decision-making powers
Austria	5 employees (on request)	Social, economic, technical and personnel policies	Social, economic, technical and personnel matters	Personnel matters
Belgium	100 employees	Social, financial and economic policies	Economic and social matters	Work regulations, recruitment, dismissals, welfare and holidays
Denmark	35 employees	Production, financial affairs, employment outlook and planned organisational change	Production, new technology and any major plans	Working conditions, personnel policy and training
Finland	30 employees	All information related to consultation issues	Plans which would have an effect on employment: dismissals, branch closing, organisational change, personnel policy and work conditions, working hours, health and safety, employment policy, training programmes, internal information and social issues	None
France	50 employees	Social balance sheet and reports on company plans, the profit and loss statement and other documents	Working conditions, training, profit-sharing plans and redundancies	Management of all company welfare schemes
Germany	5 employees (on request)	Plans for new buildings/ equipment and layout of work sites, plus information on economic and personnel policies	Safety regulations, production, recruitment, dismissals and factory organization	Social welfare, personnel policies and economic affairs
Greece	50 employees (on request)	Wide range of decisions and the progress of the business	Mass dismissals in businesses without a trade union organization	Work-place rules, health and safety, new technology, training and social activities
Hungary	50 employees	Economic and social policies	Re-organisation, privatization, rationalisation, internal regulation of working conditions	Co-decision making right, welfare, financial issues, real estate
Italy	15 employees	Investment, planning, production forecasts, technological changes, etc.	Internal work rules and the working environment	None

Table 3.1.B. **The coverage of mandated works councils** (*cont.*)

	Statutory threshold	Information entitlement	Consultation issues	Decision-making powers
Korea	30 employees	Economic matters, employment policies, safety and health issues	production, new technology, personnel matters, working condition and welfare	Company welfare schemes, training, grievances
Luxembourg	150 employees	Employment trends and the company's general progress	Plant/equipment, production and working conditions	Performance measurement, health and safety, recruitment and dismissals
Netherlands	50 employees	Employee population, financial affairs, social policies and long term plans	Economic decisions, recruitment and dismissals	Rules concerning employee benefits, working hours, holidays, health and safety, recruitment, policy regarding dismissals and training
Portugal	100 employees or 10 per cent of permanent employees on request	Internal regulations, personnel policies, production, use of labour/equipment, financial, accounting and tax affairs, general plans and reorganization	Holidays, working hours, promotions, downsizing of labour force, recruitment, bankruptcy proceedings, closing of offices or production lines, change of company seat, production and financial affairs	None
Spain	50 employees	Financial affairs, employment contracts, disciplinary actions, production, health and safety and general plans	Hours of work, dismissals, productivity, health and safety and social activities	Collective agreements

Source: Mercer and OECD.

consultation (which may be required in any case independent of any works councils) but in others agreement is required in such areas as work practices. In other countries such as the US there may be no formal requirement for councils etc, but employees participate through share schemes, with about one fifth of employees holding stock in the company in which they work. To what extent they "participate" rather than just receive dividends and capital gains will depend on the effective rights of shareholders more generally and on the details of the stock scheme (*e.g.* in some the voting rights can be exercised by management). What all these participation schemes mean for corporate governance is hard to say, in part because it is difficult to get an idea of the level of participation. Moreover, in countries with statutory participation there is no natural yardstick against which to measure the effects. This is not the case with Employee Stock Ownership Plans (ESOP). The main conclusions from 31 studies in the US are reported in Box 3.1 By and large, the effects are positive for motivation and for performance, although sometimes not in the way expected.

Box 3.1. **The positive effects of stock ownership plans**

In the US there are now a large number of studies examining the effects of employee stock ownership programmes. One survey focused on 31 of these which were based on best practice sampling techniques. Many, but not all, of the studies used multivariate analysis to hold constant the effect of other salient variables on employee attitudes or behaviour. Such analysis is particularly important for those studies which seek to examine the effect on performance. The main conclusions are:

- Most studies find higher organisational commitment and identification under employee ownership schemes, while they are mixed between favourable and neutral findings on job satisfaction, motivation, and other behavioural measures.

- There is clearly no automatic improvement of attitudes and behaviour associated with simply being an employee-shareholder.

- Where studies find improved attitudes under employee shareholder schemes, this is almost always due to the status of being an employee-owner rather than to the size of the ownership stake.

- Greater employee participation and influence in decision making may help to generate feelings of ownership, but studies are mixed on whether employee shareholders are more likely to perceive and desire a greater participation in decisions.

- Employees generally like the idea of employee shareholding.

- Studies are split between favourable and neutral findings on the relationship between employee shareholding and firm performance.

- Productivity improves by twice the average annual productivity growth in the year an ESOP is adopted and the higher productivity level is maintained in subsequent years.

- Employee shareholding is associated with greater employment stability, which does not come at the expense of lower efficiency.

- There is a higher rate of firm survival.

Source: Douglas Kruse, *Research evidence on prevalence and effects of employee ownership*, Testimony before the US House of Representatives, February 2002.

While reverse causation (*e.g.* firms with good performance introduce ESOPs) and inadequate control for industry effects[36] need to be kept in mind, the results at first sight appear puzzling: a productivity effect appears to be related not to the level of the incentive but to its existence. What appears to be at work is some kind of reputation or identification effect. There is a growing literature on this subject arguing that corporate culture as observed by the employee is important to their behaviour. Where there is identification with this culture, pay for performance does not have the observed negative relation with behaviour that goes beyond the call of duty and which is not part of the reward system.[37] Such behaviour might be more important with specialised or creative jobs, especially those involving high inputs of human capital, where options and payments in shares, or other forms of participation, are now quite common, but are often accompanied by an emphasis on the culture of the corporation. Whether participation via works councils, etc., have a similar effect as an ESOP leading to higher levels of productivity is an open question at this stage.[38]

Recent experience indicates that when all checks and balances fail, whistle-blowers have an important role to play in ensuring the proper functioning of the corporate governance system. The role of employees in recent corporate scandals – their decision as to whether or not to participate in or speak out on corporate wrong doing – was a key determinant of how the scandals unfolded. Their decisions are undoubtedly influenced by the legislative rights framework in which they operate: the existence of whistle blower protection or of effective rights to sue for undue termination of contract. The need for protection is clear: the US Commission on Public Trust and Private Enterprise reported that around 70 per cent of whistle-blowers lost their jobs or were forced to retire and in some countries disclosure by them might actually be illegal. Under the Sarbanes-Oxley Act the SEC now requires audit committees to have in place procedures for receiving complaints from whistle-blowers and in the UK, the FSA has established a telephone line and email address for employees to call the regulator about possible wrongdoing which has not been resolved internally. The Sarbanes Oxley Act protects whistle-blowers from retaliation and makes civil remedies available to them such as reinstatement, back pay and compensatory damages. In Australia there is a proposal to provide whistle-blower protection for company employees who report breaches in good faith to the corporate regulator. The need for protection is increasingly recognised in anti-corruption efforts which now highlight the role of employees' rights in combating both private and public corruption.

An issue of increasing importance is the position of pension claims on a company for defined benefit schemes, although there is also a claim where defined contribution schemes include a guaranteed minimum rate of return. Transparency is often poor allowing negotiations to proceed between management and employees without any clear indication of what it implies for the liabilities (in present value terms) of the enterprise. Accounting and actuarial standards in this area are weak and require urgent strengthening. However, for most countries the immediate problem appears to be how to protect existing claims and how to handle re-negotiation of defined benefits schemes by new owners. For example, in Australia there is now increased protection for employee entitlements in the event of insolvency: the directors are not allowed to enter into agreements or transactions for the purpose of avoiding payments of employee entitlements and the court can order compensation by directors. Whether this might result in firms declaring bankruptcy early in order to protect entitlements is an open question. In the US the problem is slightly different with concerns about moral hazard since defined benefit schemes can be insured by a federal body where the premium rates vary with the degree of under-funding but not with the actual risk of insolvency. The issue of re-negotiation of pension entitlements after a takeover has also arisen.

Balancing stakeholder claims by the management or at board level may present great difficulties suggesting that stakeholder interests might need to be more closely defined, if necessary by the law.[39] For example, the Dutch corporate governance structure has long been perceived internationally as able to balance alternative interests within the firm through its "structured regime" which involves the supervisory board taking numerous powers from shareholders. The question is how a board can balance interests while at the same time being accountable. Reflecting these concerns the social partners have now recommended to the government a major reform of the system. The new system will provide shareholders with the right to elect directors of the supervisory board and even the right to dismiss the entire board with a simple majority. The new bill also empowers employees through their Works Council to recommend, by a special nomination, one third of the candidates for the board. Interest groups will thus be more clearly defined, which will also improve the incentives for them to monitor management and to make them accountable.

In recent years there has been an increased interest in issues of corporate social responsibility. The concept is largely distinct from the stakeholder issues as treated in the Principles and generally refers to responsibly-grounded business decision making that considers the broad impact of corporate actions on people, communities, human rights, environment and health. In practice there is nevertheless an interplay between the two concepts. Thus some investors are pursuing "socially responsible investment" strategies leading to the authorities in some countries to broaden reporting requirements for both investors and operating companies (see below in transparency). Whether such "socially responsible investment" is sustainable in a market economy in the sense of profitable is a controversial question. While there are studies purporting to show excess returns for such investments, they are not as methodologically strong as the corporate governance studies discussed in Box 1.3. One reason for this is the great difficulty of measuring corporate social responsibility.[40] There have also been social activism campaigns against some companies which have certainly led to important reputational loss for the company concerned. More recently questions have been raised in the United States about the ability of companies to rebut accusations made against them in such campaigns. Many companies have now reacted to the changing sentiment by establishing company codes of conduct and in some cases by opening overseas supply chains to audit. Company ethical codes are also claimed to help eliminate company conduct that is too close to the line of illegality. The more important issue of compliance itself is taken up in the final section on the duties of the board. As noted below, there is also a move towards greater disclosure by enterprises about how their operations directly affect the environment.

Better disclosure and transparency

A great deal of activity in member countries and concern on the part of observers has revolved around the question of disclosure and transparency. Aspects related to remuneration are handled in the following section on the operations of the board. Disclosure should cover the material matters of the corporation including "*major share ownership and voting rights, material foreseeable risk factors, material issues regarding employees and other stakeholders, and governance structures and policies*". Most importantly, Principle IV.B of the Principles states that "*information should be prepared, audited and disclosed in accordance with high quality standards of accounting, financial and non-financial disclosure, and audit*". Moreover, (IV.C), "*an annual audit should be conducted by an independent auditor in order to provide an external and objective assurance on the way in which financial statements have been prepared and presented*".

Disclosure is not simply related to the frequency of corporate financial reports, about which there is a wide range of opinion,[41] but as the Principles point out it is a matter of timeliness. Countries vary quite a lot in specifying when market related information should be disclosed. Australia has a mandatory continuous disclosure system to ensure that investors have equal access to information that materially impacts on prices of traded securities. Continuous disclosure is also intended to ensure that securities prices reflect as closely as possible their underlying value. Nevertheless, reflecting the move toward better enforcement in other countries, the authorities are now proposing to increase penalties and to clarify compensation rights for breaching continuous disclosure requirements.

Toward better financial and accounting standards

A major problem in fulfilling the content of the Principles has been the need for improved accounting standards in most member countries (Box 3.2), particularly in the area of contingent liabilities, and off-balance sheet arrangements, including the consolidation of entities that facilitate such arrangements. The true extent of pension liabilities was poorly reflected in company accounts during the 1990s in, *inter alia*, the Netherlands, Germany and Japan, although since 2000 there has been major progress in addressing the issue. National systems, however, continue to differ in the choice of discount rate and the amortisation period for any under-funding (Box 3.2). To give an idea of the sums involved, one analyst has estimated that 80 of the largest 100 companies in the UK had pension deficits amounting to £50 billion, approximately equal to their annual profits.[42] In the US, optimistic assumptions about the rate of return on pension fund assets made during a period of unusually positive market performance resulted in companies booking substantial income into their ordinary operating profits. In assessing the financial implications of pension schemes a great deal will depend on the rules applying to the work of the actuary. In the UK, the independence of the actuaries has been called into question.[43] Equally important has been the failure to adequately recognise the cost of stock options. The net result of these weaknesses is that the actual position of insiders *vis-à-vis* shareholders, employees and creditors has not been transparent and therefore the system of checks and balances might have been impaired.

In this context, the decision by the EU and Australia to adopt International Accounting Standards will be important since IAS is based on principles which the authorities believe should provide better coverage in these three poorly defined areas. However, a great deal will depend on whether the key principles will not become weaker in the process of international negotiations, especially in the area of options and derivatives accounting and whether application of the principles will be consistent and enforceable. It is argued by some professional observers[44] that the US system should redress the balance in favour of principles rather than rules and there is a process in place to encourage convergence of the standards of the International Accounting Standards Board (IASB) and those in the US. But again much will depend on whether the advantages of principles will be diluted by the advent of rules about how to interpret the provisions, especially with respect to minimising the risks of litigation through the establishment of safe harbours and "bright lines".

An important issue concerns how to implement reporting about material risk factors. The Principles argue that material information on foreseeable risk factors (including issues concerning employees and stakeholders) should also be disclosed and this line of reasoning is reflected in many national principles

Box 3.2. **Major issues in accounting principles**

Regardless of whether an accounting system is principles or rules-based, and to what degree, there are a number of issues which need to be dealt with covering both the balance sheet and the profit and loss account. Some of these issues have arisen due to more complex financial instruments coming onto the market. Three specific areas have been the source of recent and potential problems: pension accounting for systems with both defined benefit and defined contribution schemes, the treatment of stock options, and balance sheet issues and income recognition questions arising from full, fair value accounting.[1]

In countries with defined benefit schemes (or in those with defined contribution plans but subject to a minimum rate of return guarantee) there is an issue about how to value pension assets and liabilities. For example, pension fund assets in the UK have to be marked to market value (this is also the case in many other countries) while the AA corporate bond yield is used as the discount rate on pension fund liabilities. The current low level of interest rates aggravates the funding gap. In some other countries, companies have greater discretion in reporting pension liabilities by varying the actuarial assumptions, discount rate or the rate of return assumptions in their calculations. Moreover, the consequences from changes in the assumptions are often averaged and the period required to fully fund or amortise any deficit varies quite widely, up to some 15 years. Uncertainty about the true value of "hidden" pension liabilities has led leading rating agencies to propose company downgrades in some countries which have proved controversial.

Economic principles call for the expensing of stock options since an issue is associated with a cost in the same way as a free distribution of shares, albeit contingent on the option being exercised: once exercised they constitute a real wealth transfer to the beneficiaries at the expense of other stockholders.[2] It is true that an individual option might not be exercised but in the late 1990s it appears that most were eventually exercised and with weaker market conditions in recent years many have been re-priced so that they might well be exercised at some date in the future. In any case, many other costs are also uncertain or contingent but are still taken into account in determining current profitability. How to cost options remains an issue which has contributed to delay in deciding whether to expense them, not to mention strong opposition from some sectors. There are three methods available with very different results.[3] According to one study covering 325 large American firms in 2000, the reduction in reported profits ranges from 5 per cent to 22 per cent depending on the method used to cost options. It should also be noted that more important expenses such as depreciation are also subject to a high level of uncertainty.

Box 3.2. **Major issues in accounting principles** (cont.)

More important than determining an estimated cost, however, is that lack of expensing may have led to a situation of "never measured, never managed". In addition to lack of expensing, favourable tax treatment, especially with respect to executive remuneration in the US, has also contributed to the popularity of options, even though practice indicates that the incentive effects are often distorted. Holding shares directly might be a more transparent and powerful form of incentive for aligning the interests of management with shareholders in the longer run.[4] Some large entities in the US have simultaneously reported high losses for tax purposes, since options are treated as a tax deduction, but high profits for accounting purposes because they are not expensed. Outside the US, in some jurisdictions there is not even a disclosure standard.

Fair value or mark to market accounting is a fairly standard economic concept but is also proving a fertile area for abuse. Many standard setters recognize that mark to market across the whole balance sheet can open the door to more manipulation than it closes and the problem will need to be dealt with. Some companies may discount very long-term streams of estimated income into the present using proprietary models, and add the resultant calculation to current year's profit. Income recognition is thus pushed to the limit and this is even more so if prices are drawn from thin and illiquid markets such as the market for fibre-optic capacity. Lower interest rates during the past decade and more advanced securitization techniques have also meant that more and more of the future margin might have been discounted to the present. Some widely used stock valuation techniques apply a multiple to earnings, which are in fact already discounted.

Excessive discounting also affects the balance sheet as does inadequate pension accounting. Other accounting issues have also come up including the practice of leasing equipment to keep it off the balance sheet. This is important in the airline and telecommunication sectors. Some have proposed a simple rule: all contractual obligations and all non-cancellable leases must be capitalised. Finally, the consolidation standard for balance sheets has been a major problem highlighted in the Enron case, even though the company actually violated the existing rules. Setting numerical thresholds appears to have led to aggressive accounting, which perhaps might be avoided by the use of principles such as effective control.

1. For more detailed arguments see J. Caruana *et al.*, Enron *et al.*, *Market Forces in Disarray*, Group of Thirty, Washington, 2002.
2. For examples of the economic cost see R. Bliss, "Common sense about executive stock options", *Chicago Fed Letter*, 188, April 2003.
3. The three different methods for valuing the total cost of options are: the value of options issued during a given accounting year calculated using the Black-Sholes model of option pricing; the cost of all outstanding options if they were "immunised" by the company buying identical options in the market; and the full cost which is the change in the value of all outstanding options plus the cost of those exercised during the year.
4. For a detailed discussion about the specifics of options which can lead to incentives for management not to act in the longer run interests of shareholders and others see Bebchuk, *et al.*, *op. cit.*, and Graef Crystal, *The Perfect Stock Option Plan*, Paper prepared for the Californian State Teachers' Retirement System, February 2003.

and codes. However, implementation does beg the question of defining materiality and standards in these areas are much less developed than is the case with straightforward financial disclosure. For example, as in many countries, the Combined Code in the UK recommends that the board should present a balanced and understandable assessment of the company's position and prospects while the UK's company law review identified items that should be disclosed if directors consider them material. In order to give content to such recommendations, a working group has been set up to develop broad principles and practical guidance on how directors can assess whether an item is material. The efforts in the UK to improve disclosure, which will require additional reporting requirements, has been accompanied by a Regulatory Impact Assessment that considers the costs of the various options and the likely benefits.[45]

... with important implications for incentives facing accountants and auditors

Although problems concerning external auditors in the US have made the greatest headlines, a number of other member countries are in the process of tightening standards in the light of domestic experience. For example, in Ireland a Review Group on Auditing identified a number of problems in the regulation and operation of the auditing and accounting profession as early as July 2000. A new bill is to be introduced to parliament in 2003 that will enhance self-regulation by the creation of a specialised supervisory authority and strengthen the independence of auditors. Members of the EU also have to adapt their systems in line with a Commission Recommendation issued in May 2002 which prohibits auditors from carrying out an audit required by law if they have any relationship with the client that might compromise their independence, notably any financial, employment or other link, or any situation where the auditors provide to the same client services additional to the audit. Since the beginning of 2002, audit firms and natural persons in Austria must be rotated every six years. Auditors are presumed to have lost independence when more than 30 per cent of their income over the previous five years is derived from consulting or auditing a company and its subsidiaries. Implementation of the Commission's Recommendation appears to differ across members of the EU so that while all are moving in the same direction they are not necessarily harmonising approaches.[46] Japan is also enhancing auditor oversight and independence with the passing of a bill by the Diet in May 2003. The Certified Public Accountants and Auditing Oversight Board is to be established to monitor the quality of the review process which, as before, is undertaken by the professional body, the Japanese Institute of Certified Public Accountants.

CORPORATE GOVERNANCE: A SURVEY OF OECD COUNTRIES – ISBN 92-64-10605-7 – © OECD 2004

The process of setting new international standards covering auditor independence and audit quality is also now underway, the latter being driven to some extent by the realisation that the four large international accounting and audit companies are not in fact a guarantee of uniform quality standards across countries. The International Organisation of Securities Commissions (IOSCO) has released principles covering auditor independence and auditor oversight.[47] The principles are based on what appears to be a growing consensus among securities regulators as to the nature of the threats to an auditor's independence and the limitations on the extent to which those threats can be mitigated by voluntarily applied safeguards of various types. Moreover, there is general agreement among IOSCO regulators that the simple establishment of standards governing auditor independence is not sufficient, in itself, to provide assurance that auditors are in fact independent. Any standards must be supported by rigorous requirements for audit firms to establish and maintain internal systems and processes for monitoring, identifying and addressing threats to independence. Such internal systems related to independence must be assessed and evaluated by external oversight bodies of which there are two: an audit committee or some equivalent in the firm being audited (see below) and a professional oversight body that acts and is seen to act in the public interest. The IOSCO principles are summarised in Box 3.3. Finally, standards for the audit process itself are being reviewed by the International Auditing and Assurance Standards Board (IAASB). As the IAASB is an industry group there have been calls by IOSCO, the Financial Stability Forum and others to subject the standard setting process to some form of international public interest oversight.

Changes in the way accounting and auditing firms operate in the US have moved quite quickly and are far reaching (Box 3.4). They do, however, involve fundamental issues for other countries, especially with respect to the registration and oversight of foreign auditors which audit companies whose securities are listed in the US, with the new Public Company Accounting Oversight Board (PCAOB). While recognising the importance of audit work papers to effective auditor oversight, concerns have been raised about the US authorities' access to a foreign firm's audit work papers. The PCAOB along with the SEC are now considering these issues and discussions are taking place with concerned countries. As noted above, these discussions are taking place against the background of a broader process to enhance auditor oversight throughout the OECD area and elsewhere. The PCAOB's requirements also concern the relationship of the external auditor with the company. The issues are discussed further in the section on board functions and audit committees.

.3. The IOSCO principles covering national standards on auditor independence and external oversight

According to IOSCO, national standards of auditor independence should:

- Establish a framework of principles supported by a combination of prohibitions, restrictions and other policies and procedures and disclosures that address at least the threats to independence arising from self interest, self review, advocacy, familiarity and intimidation.

- Identify appropriate safeguards that the auditor should implement in order to mitigate threats to independence that arise from permissible activities and relationships.

- Require the auditor to identify and evaluate all significant or potentially significant threats to independence, including those arising from recent relationships with the entity being audited that may have preceded the appointment as auditor, and document how the auditor has applied safeguards to mitigate those threats.

- The securities market regulators should ensure that there is a system in place to require prompt disclosure of information about the replacement of an auditor of a listed entity.

To back-up these standards for auditor independence, IOSCO calls for member jurisdictions to provide:

- A mechanism to provide that a body acting in the public interest will provide oversight of the quality and implementation of auditing, independence, and ethical standards, as well as audit quality control environments.

- A mechanism should exist to require auditors to be subject to the discipline of an auditor oversight body that is independent of the audit profession, or, if a professional body acts as the oversight body, is overseen by an independent body. Such an auditor oversight body must operate in the public interest, and have an appropriate membership, an adequate charter of responsibilities and powers, and adequate funding that is not under the control of the auditing profession, to carry out those responsibilities.

- An auditor oversight body should establish a process for performing regular reviews of audit procedures and practices of firms that audit the financial statements of listed public companies.

- The oversight body should also address questions such as professional competency, rotation of audit personnel, consulting and other non-audit services.

- The body should have the authority to stipulate remedial measures for problems detected, and to initiate and/or carry out disciplinary proceedings to impose sanctions on auditors and audit firms, as appropriate.

CORPORATE GOVERNANCE: A SURVEY OF OECD COUNTRIES – ISBN 92-64-10605-7 – © OECD 2004

Box 3.4. **Implementing the Sarbanes-Oxley Act: Decisions by the SEC**

Rules Strengthening Auditor Independence

Non-Audit Services that are prohibited

- Bookkeeping or other services related to accounting records or financial statements.
- Financial information system design and implementation consulting.
- Appraisal or valuation services, fairness opinions, or contribution-in-kind reports.
- Actuarial services.
- Internal audit outsourcing services.
- Management functions or human resources services.
- Broker/dealer, investment adviser, or investment banking services.
- Legal services.
- Expert services unrelated to the audit.

Audit Committee Pre-Approval of Services Provided by Auditor

- Audit committee must pre-approve allowable audit and non-audit services to be provided by the auditor of the issuer's financial statements.

Disclosures to Investors of Services Provided by the Auditor

Disclosure of services approved by the audit committee will be required in their annual report with fees disclosed for the categories of services:

- Audit services.
- Audit related services.
- Tax services.
- Other services.

Permitted Non-audit Service: Tax Service

- Tax service is not expressly prohibited subject to audit committee pre-approval.
- Accordingly, accountants will still be able to provide tax compliance, tax planning, and tax advice to audit clients when those services have been approved by the issuer's audit committee.
- Some tax services could impair independence such as representing a client in tax court and these would be prohibited.

Box 3.4. **Implementing the Sarbanes-Oxley Act: Decisions by the SEC** *(cont.)*

Audit Partner Rotation

- The lead and concurring partner must be subject to rotation after five years with a five year time-out period.

- Other audit partners are subject to rotation after seven years with a two year time-out.

Cooling Off Period

- A one-year cooling off period before a member of the audit engagement team may accept employment with the client.

Auditor Communication With Audit Committee

- Accounting firms will be required to report all critical accounting policies and practices used by the issuer.

- Accounting firms will be required to report all material alternative accounting treatments of financial information within generally accepted accounting principles (GAAP) that have been discussed with management.

- Accounting firm is required to communicate material written communications with management.

Small business/Small Firm Consideration

Those audit firms with fewer than five audit clients and fewer than ten partners may be exempt from the partner rotation and compensation provisions provided each engagement is subject to special review by the Public Company Accounting Oversight Board at least every three years.

Foreign Considerations

- Additional time will be afforded to foreign accounting firms with respect to compliance with rotation requirements.

Rules on Disclosure of Off-Balance Sheet Arrangements and Aggregate Contractual Obligations

Require each annual financial report filed with the SEC, to disclose all material off-balance sheet transactions, arrangements, obligations (including contingent obligations) and other relationships of the issuer with unconsolidated entities or other persons, that may have a material current or future effect on financial condition, changes in financial condition, results of operations, liquidity, capital expenditures, capital resources, or significant components of revenues or expenses. This would include:

- Guarantee contracts.

- Retained or contingent interests in assets transferred to an unconsolidated entity.

> ### Box 3.4. **Implementing the Sarbanes-Oxley Act: Decisions by the SEC** (cont.)
>
> - Derivative instruments that are classified as equity.
> - Material variable interest in unconsolidated entities that conduct certain activities.
> - Disclosure will be principles-based to require registrant to provide such other information that it believes is necessary for an understanding of its off-balance sheet arrangements and their specified material effects.
>
> **Rules on Retention of Records Relevant to Audits and Reviews**
>
> Auditors will be required to retain documents for a period of 7 years. Documents include:
>
> - Correspondence and work papers.
> - Communications.
> - Analysis.
> - Any other financial date related to the audit or review.

Improving non-financial disclosure

The Principles argue that material information on foreseeable risk factors and issues regarding employees and stakeholders should also be disclosed. This line of reasoning is now reflected in many national principles and codes. However, implementation does beg the question of defining materiality and standards in these areas are much less developed than is the case with financial disclosure. Although some countries require disclosure of information regarding human resource policies, standards remain under-developed. This situation has led the UK authorities to establish a committee to examine how to improve reporting about human capital management and how a progressive improvement in reporting standards can best be encouraged.[48] Reflecting the broader debate, the committee will also investigate how such disclosure can be audited.

In a number of countries the question of reporting broader social and environmental issues, and how this can best be done, remains on the agenda. Indeed, in May 2001 French corporate law was amended to require listed companies to disclose in their annual reports how they take the social and environmental consequences of their activities into account.[49] A handful of international standards and codes have contributed guidance of a voluntary and non-binding character, which may be useful as enterprises develop their own policies.[50] The OECD *Guidelines for Multinational Enterprises,* in its disclosure chapter states that enterprises are encouraged to communicate additional information that could include: "Value statements or statements of business conduct intended for public disclosure including information on the social, ethical and environmental policies of the enterprise and other codes of conduct to which the company subscribes." The formulation in the OECD *Guidelines* preserves a broad range of choice and flexibility for enterprises considering how to report on social and environmental issues. In a study of 100 multinational enterprises prepared by the OECD in 2003 around 95 of them had made policy statements on the environment and health and safety, 80 on labour relations and 45 on anti-corruption, integrity and transparency.[51] An important development is that the demand for broader reporting has been accompanied by suggestions about how company reporting can be verified.[52]

The Principles call for the disclosure of material information about governance structures and policies. A number of national principles now include such a requirement to be issued with the annual reports. While experience with such reporting is still limited, one study of Canadian firms has found that the quality of disclosure has been perfunctory.

Getting the boards to improve the oversight of management

With unitary board systems a tension is sometimes observed between the view that the board should contribute contacts, resources and skills to the operation of the company, and the position that the board is primarily in place to monitor the management. The two views have different implications for the structure of the board, the former arguing for a greater share of insiders relative to outsiders.[53] The Principles make a more nuanced case by specifying that the board is chiefly responsible for monitoring managerial performance and achieving an adequate rate of return for shareholders, while preventing conflicts of interest and balancing competing demands on the company. Most important of all, the board is responsible for guiding corporate strategy. In two tier board systems, the question of composition does not arise (*i.e.* the supervisory board is by law non-executive) although the degree to which it can and should guide corporate strategy and balance interests is often debated. Also debated is whether the absence of executives limits their access to information and restrains informed debate, and at the end of the day could lead to ineffective monitoring. This is an issue in Germany, leading the authorities to introduce a self-check system (see above) for supervisory boards.[54] However, the unwieldy size of supervisory boards also needs to be addressed. With the EU now offering companies the choice of one or two tier systems for companies registering under European statutes (*societas europaea*),[55] the advantages and disadvantages of the two systems is once more open to debate. France is the first to give companies such a choice and Italy is following suit with three choices.

The Principles specify that the board should fulfil certain key functions (Chapter V.D) including selecting and compensating key executives, controlling conflicts of interest and ensuring the integrity of the accounting and financial reporting systems. Experience over the past two years has affirmed that this list is appropriate and indeed it is often recognised in national laws. However, effective implementation on a day to day basis has been found wanting in a number of countries stimulating the proposed actions discussed below. The Principles also call on the board to monitor the effectiveness of the governance practices under which it operates and make changes as needed. As noted above, Germany has now mandated such a review exercise (it is also recommended in the UK Code) and a number of voluntary principles and codes call for the company to make a statement about its corporate governance practices.

Towards "independent" and more effective boards

The Principles assign an important place to the responsibilities of the board in overseeing management and fulfilling its accountability obligations to the company and the shareholders. This has important implications for the nature of the board members: *The board should be able to exercise objective judgement on corporate affairs, independent, in particular from management:*

1. *Boards should consider assigning a sufficient number of non-executive board members capable of exercising independent judgement to tasks where there is a potential conflict of interest. Examples of such key responsibilities are financial reporting, nomination and executive and board remuneration.*

2. *Board members should devote sufficient time to their responsibilities.*

3. *In order to fulfil their responsibilities, board members should have access to accurate, relevant and timely information.*

In several countries the thrust of recent proposals or actual changes has been toward increasing not only the number of non-executive directors (which do appear to make a difference, Box 3.5) but also ensuring that they are "independent". For example, the Commission on Public Trust and Private Enterprise (US) recommends that boards should have a substantial majority of independent directors and the listing requirements of the NYSE envisage a majority. The recent Higgs report (UK) proposes that at least half the company board, excluding the chairman, comprise "independent" non-executive directors. The Sarbanes-Oxley Act mandates "independent" audit boards but does not refer to the board as a whole. And in Japan, the new company law allows firms to choose between two models (the *kansayaku* and a single tier board with committees) for their boards and increases the role for more clearly defined "outsiders" who should never have worked for the firm or its subsidiaries.[56]

Box 3.5. **Board composition matters: some empirical evidence**

The question whether board composition, and in particular the presence of non-executive directors (outside directors), leads to better enterprise performance is one where judgments vary widely and the econometric evidence is contradictory if not negative.[1] This is hardly surprising since performance will depend on many factors outside the control of the board which is in any case there to monitor and appoint management rather than take commercial decisions. Dynamics should also be taken into account in assessing the role of boards but this is rather complex with the available data. For example, an outsider board may be more inclined to change management but results may take some time to emerge and might even worsen at first as past errors are written off. Moreover, the board is also in place to control risk and prevent corporate disasters. A number of studies therefore focus on decisions or actions taken by the board and the better ones try and account for the fact that the board is itself related to enterprise performance. These studies do indeed suggest an important role for board composition.

A survey by Hermalin and Weisbach[2] mainly of US studies found no relationship of board composition (the proportion of non-executive directors or outsiders) to performance. However, board composition appears to affect the quality of decisions on CEO replacement, responses to a hostile takeover, adoption of a poison pill and the design of CEO compensation schemes. In boards dominated by outside directors, CEO turnover is more sensitive to firm performance and a CEO is more likely to be replaced by someone outside the firm than in companies with dominant insiders. The stock market reaction to poison pills is positive, presumably indicating that they are seen as a bargaining tool for a higher price rather than as a sign of entrenchment. Moreover, measured in terms of the fall in share price by acquiring firms, it appears that the market perceives that firms with outsider boards make better acquisitions (or at least less bad ones). However, it is not just a matter of having outsiders *per se* on the board. The relation between CEO turnover and firm performance is stronger when the outside directors are paid using incentives. On the other hand, the qualities of an outsider are also important. CEO pay rises with the number of outside directors appointed by the CEO and the number of busy directors, where the latter is defined by the number of additional directorships held by a director. CEO pay also increases when a board contains interlocking directors who, it might be supposed, are more likely to be influenced by the CEO. Board dynamics are also important suggesting an important role for board independence (which is unobservable) from the CEO and the existence of a bargaining framework between the two. Where the CEO has a major role in the board selection process or when the CEO is on the nominating committee, the number of outside directors is subsequently lower. After a period of good performance the CEO tends to add more insiders to the board.

Box 3.5. **Board composition matters:
some empirical evidence** (*cont.*)

Whether independent boards will perform any better than outsider boards will take some time to emerge and will have to be tested with information about members which is often not currently available.

A study for the UK (Dahya *et al.*, 2002) looks at the experience with the 1992 Cadbury Code of Best Practice which recommended that boards include at least three outside directors and that the role of CEO and chairman be split. One school of thought would expect no change since market forces should have propelled boards toward efficient structures. However, the study found that the negative relationship between CEO turnover and performance became stronger following the Code's issuance and this was concentrated in firms which adopted the Code. No connection was found with profitability.

1. For a condensed overview see M. Becht, P. Bolton, and A. Röell, "Corporate Governance and Control", *ECGI Working Paper*, 2002.
2. B. Hermalin and M. Weisbach, "Boards of directors as an endogenously determined institution: A survey of the economic literature", *NBER Working Paper*, 8161, 2001.

Two inter-related questions are crucial: are "independent" directors an appropriate response to the evidence of agency costs and inadequate monitoring noted above and if so, how can the concept be made operational? Independent directors are argued to have an important role in monitoring and controlling conflicts of interest on the part of executive directors and management. As such they are put forward as suitable directors to deal with compensation, audits, and nomination questions, particularly in the US. Such situations would call for independence from management, a definition also noted in the Principles. However, at least twelve national principles are also concerned with independence from a major shareholder underlining the reality that in many countries there is a strong relation between management and a major shareholder. While individuals might well start as "independent", can they be expected to remain so (except formally) after they have become members of the "board team" that from the efficiency point of view is claimed to be important. Moreover, as their remuneration will have to increase in line with the new responsibilities and work load, isn't there a danger that they will become "dependent" on the one firm?

The incentive for the independent director to retain independence of judgement is the key factor and this would appear to come down to how they are selected or nominated in the first place, as well as the strength of any reputation effect. A director with a clear mandate from shareholders (or stakeholders) might be expected to remain more independently minded than one elected from a broad slate of candidates put forward by, for example, a CEO. There are other incentive effects, which in the meantime are well known and accepted in some companies: a director should be able to hold shares in a company (or even be partly paid with shares, not options) but with a commitment not to sell them for the period in office. This at least appears to better align incentives with shareholders. But is it wise to define independence in part by reference to the number of shares held even if the definition refers in the first instance to a safe harbour?[57] The question of independent directors can even be stood on its head: is there a requirement for more "dependent" directors: directors who owe their election to particular groups of shareholders or even stakeholders? This can also be viewed from the perspective of better representation. In some countries it is already clear, for example, that certain directors in fact "represent" the dominant shareholders. In these instances, the presence of "independent" directors may be that of protecting minority shareholders. For example, the fund management association in Italy has called for the new corporate law to give minority shareholders the right to nominate directors in all listed companies. The danger is, however, that as the members of the board come to represent constituencies, the danger of inequitable treatment and insider trading might increase. This makes it all the more important to provide for proper safeguards and to enforce them appropriately.

The issue of representation occurs immediately when it is necessary to implement the concept of independence. The Higgs Report seeks to give an operational definition (Box 3.6) which excludes directors who "represent" a significant shareholder, but unlike the NYSE and Nasdaq does not set a limit on their own shareholdings. The requirement may make sense in a voting system which allows a major shareholder to dominate but does raise questions about the election system itself. It is informative to note that the Higgs report also calls for a senior independent director to be nominated to deal with shareholders, if they have concerns that have not been resolved through the normal channels of contact with the chairman or chief executive. Similarly, the US Commission on Public Trust and Private Enterprise which advocates independent directors, also calls for ways for "significant long term shareholders to nominate directors". The designation "long term" does, however, raise issues of equitable treatment.

There have also been moves to improve both the quality of the board and the information it receives. In the UK, the Higgs report showed dissatisfaction with the quality of non-executive directors and called upon companies to set aside adequate resources and ensure sufficient time for them to become familiar with the company and with their duties. Rather surprisingly, the report found through its commissioned research and interviews that there was a lack of clarity about the role of the non-executive director and that the

Box 3.6. **What is an independent director?: one definition**

The Higgs report states "that a non-executive director is considered independent when the board determines that the director is independent in character and judgement and there are no relationships or circumstances which could affect, or appear to affect, the director's judgement".

Such relationships or circumstances would include where the director:

- is a former employee of the company or group until five years after employment (or any other material connection has ended);
- has, or has had within the last three years, a material business relationship with the company either directly, or as a partner, shareholder or director or senior employee of a body that has such a relationship with the company;
- has received or receives additional remuneration from the company apart from a directors fee, participates in the company's share option or a performance related pay scheme, or is a member of the company's pension scheme;
- has close family ties with any of the company's advisers, directors or senior employees;
- holds cross directorships or has significant links with other directors through involvement in other companies or bodies;
- represents a significant shareholder; or
- has served on the board for more than ten years.

The board should identify in its annual report the non-executive directors it determines to be independent. The board should state its reasons if a director is considered to be independent notwithstanding the existence of relationships or circumstances which may appear relevant to its determination.

Source: Review of the role and effectiveness of non-executive directors, DTI London, 2003 (otherwise known as the Higgs Report).

current British code offered little guidance.[58] In addition, the report noted that boards tended to be recruited from a very small population of acceptable candidates (leading one journalist to note that the base for selecting directors is pale, male and stale!). This prompted the government to ask another institution to establish a wider base of potential candidates. Why it should do this and not leave it to recruitment companies is not clear.[59] In Norway, there is now a requirement for the board to achieve a specific gender balance and in Swedish companies with state participation the ratio is nearly 40 per cent.

Another issue touched on in the annotations to the Principles is the role of the Chairman of the board and this has received increased attention in a number of countries with unitary boards. However, opinions remain widely divided. The argument put forward most forcefully in the British context is that separation (with the chairman also independent) would help ensure an appropriate balance of power, increased accountability, and enhanced capacity of the board for independent decision making.[60] This is opposed by many in the US and France (where the *PdG* has a long tradition). Even though the recent Commission on Public Trust proposed a separation, there was also a strong dissenting opinion and no other principles and codes in the US have gone as far as recommending a split.[61] Such a point of view expresses the understandable concern to avoid increased board bureaucracy which could stifle entrepreneurial flare.[62] Nevertheless, even those opposed to separation see the need to give the Board more structure. For example, independent or non-executive directors should be able to meet separately under some lead director who can then channel opinions to the Chairman/CEO. The dissenting vote on the Commission noted that it was already the practice of well governed American boards for the non-executive directors to meet privately presided over by the independent board member who chairs the governance or nominating committee. In systems with two tier boards, an issue which has arisen in some countries (*e.g.* Germany) is whether it is appropriate for the chairman of the management board to become chairman of the supervisory board on retirement from the former.

Board structure and the execution of key tasks

In fulfilling its key duties to review executive and board remuneration, ensuring a formal and transparent board nomination process and ensuring the integrity of the company's accounting and reporting system, there has been a tendency in a number of countries to give the board more structure. This often involves some form of sub-committee although there are key differences between whether they serve simply a consultative function or whether their delegated tasks are binding on the board. With or without such structure, the importance of the tasks is emphasised in many countries, but it is also probably an area where implementation has been weakest.

Executive compensation

One of the most controversial issues noted above in recent years has been the matter of executive compensation. The Principles cover the issue in several sections: Disclosure and transparency, IV.A.4: *Disclosure should include Members of the board and key executives, and their remuneration*, and; under Responsibility of the Board, V.E.1 it is recommended that "*non-executive board members capable of independent judgement*" take on the responsibility of setting executive and board remuneration. The annotation calls for disclosure to cover individuals and details of performance based schemes: *Companies are generally expected to disclose sufficient information on the remuneration of board members and key executives (either individually or in the aggregate) for investors to properly assess the costs and benefits of remuneration plans and the contribution of incentive schemes, such as stock option schemes, to performance.*

In the wake of recent scandals, a number of countries have moved to enforce better disclosure of board and executive compensation, and a small although increasing number also call for individual remuneration packages to be published. CEOs and other leading executives and board members are often in a unique position to abuse their position of power and in several countries this has come as a surprise to governments, the public and shareholders. It is therefore important not only to publish individual remuneration but to make the definition as broad as possible so as to avoid better camouflaged pay structures with sub-optimal incentives. The experience indicates that details of the compensation schemes are as important as the overall level in assessing the incentive structure and that remuneration also includes pension schemes, termination benefits and golden parachutes. The last two have become topical in a number of countries (*e.g.* Germany, France, UK) especially where large termination benefits have been associated with poor company performance. The situation has led to calls for legislation although it is not at all clear whether this is an appropriate response in view of the complexities of executive contracts and the specific needs of firms.[63] Moreover, information about the structure of stock option schemes is also crucial in assessing the incentive structure.[64]

Moving beyond disclosure as a governance tool, in an increasing number of countries there are also moves to find more structural solutions, supported if necessary by guidelines (Box 3.7). Compensation or remuneration committees are either being established or strengthened by the inclusion of independent members. For example, both the New York Stock Exchange and Nasdaq have proposed independent compensation committees as part of their listing requirements and codes and principles in many other countries go in the same direction. The potential for conflicts of interest in the current system is made clear by a report for the United States which indicates that of the largest 2000 corporations, 420 of them had compensation committees in 2001 with members who had business ties or other relations with the chief executive or the company.[65] However, "independence" *per se* is no panacea: one study finds that CEO compensation is higher when more of the outside directors are appointed by the CEO, when the outside directors are older and when they serve on five or more boards, and when the board contains interlocking directors.[66] Institutional investors and large blockholders also have a crucial role to play even in markets with more dispersed ownership. Indeed, a number of organisations have now established codes of best practice specifying how they

> ## Box 3.7. **Guidelines for executive compensation packages**
>
> Guidelines concerning executive remuneration packages have been drawn up by a number of organisations in the OECD area. An example which also illustrates the difficulty in making guidelines too detailed in the context of an active market for managerial talent is the proposal of the Investment and Financial Services Association in Australia. The key principles are:
>
> - Executive remuneration should realistically reflect the responsibilities of executives.
>
> - Remuneration should be reasonable and comparable with market standards.
>
> - Incentive schemes should be clearly linked to performance benchmarks.
>
> - Shareholders should be informed so that they can decide if the schemes are reasonable.
>
> - Boards should develop appropriate performance hurdles that focus on actual company performance (*e.g.* long term growth).

will approach the key question of remuneration.[67] Improved transparency will also allow such shareholders to make more effective use of their power, something which has been observed recently in the UK.

Regulating conflict of interest...

The Principles cover the broad issue of conflict of interest under several headings: Equitable treatment of shareholders, II.B; *Insider trading should be prohibited.* II.C, *Members of the board and managers should be required to disclose any material interests in transactions or matters affecting the corporation*; and, The responsibilities of the board, V.D.4, *Monitoring and managing potential conflicts of interest of management, board members and shareholders, including misuse of corporate assets and abuse in related party transactions.*

This area, touching as it does on ethics, has been emphasised by the various codes and principles (Table 2.2). In dealing with the most egregious abuses, insider-trading laws have been implemented in all OECD countries mainly during the 1990s but the indicators are that their enforcement appears to have been quite modest.[68] In some countries such as Germany, voluntary codes were first implemented but proved ineffective.

In many cases, the issue comes down to proper conduct and while some codes have proposed a board member to oversee ethics (in Germany a compliance commissioner has been proposed by the Berlin Initiative Code who would also be a member of the supervisory board), the question of what

> ### Box 3.8. **An example of a code of conduct covering conflict of interest**
>
> The Berlin Initiative Group as part of their suggested code of corporate governance proposed:
>
> - Members of the Management Board (the lower board in a two tier system) always remain personally loyal to their company.
>
> - Members of the Management Board in particular may neither directly nor indirectly through persons connected with them, take advantage of the company's business chances, assist competitors or undertake commercial transactions with the company which do not correspond with normal market conditions.
>
> - Participation by members of the Management Board in other companies must be revealed to the Chairman of the Supervisory Board and has to be examined for any possible conflict of interest.
>
> - The chairman of the Supervisory Board must approve acceptance of a seat on the supervisory board of another company, as well as engaging in significant ancillary activities.
>
> - The Management Board will appoint a representative who issues guidelines for the sale and purchase of shares in the company and who supervises their operation. All members of the Management Board will acknowledge in writing the rules applicable for insider dealings as well as these guidelines.

the code should comprise has been left open. The Berlin Code provides an example which is clearly structured and precisely worded given the complexity of the issues involved (Box 3.8).

... and ensuring ethical standards

With respect to ethical behaviour, the Principles mainly focus on compliance with existing laws: III.A, *The corporate governance framework should assure that the rights of stakeholders that are protected by law are respected*; III.B, *Where stakeholder interests are protected by law, stakeholders should have the opportunity to obtain effective redress for violation of their rights*; V.C, *The board should ensure compliance with applicable law and take into account the interests of stakeholders*. The OECD *Guidelines for Multinational Enterprises* is more specific in its recommendations and in some cases covers issues not covered by national laws. The areas covered by the *Guidelines* are general policies, employment and industrial relations practices, environment, combating bribery, science and technology, taxation, disclosure, consumer interests and competition.[69]

Compliance with existing laws and regulations has become a major concern in a number of countries together with promoting ethical behaviour. National principles often call for a code of company ethics to be developed and disclosed by the board which includes compliance (*e.g.* NYSE listing requirements). In a number of cases there is also a call for an ethics committee of the board to be established or for a board member to take responsibility for overseeing the code. It appears that many companies see ethical codes or company codes of conduct as a way to prevent abuses of market power and behaviour that approaches too closely to the point of committing illegal conduct, and to act as ethical guidelines in the decision making process. As one review notes, the codes reflect a variety of legal, regulatory and social pressures.[70] Most company codes include provisions on environmental policies, labour management, bribery and corruption prohibitions, consumer protection, scientific and technological advancements and disclosure. In drawing up company codes, international standards have clearly been important, especially the *OECD Guideline for Multinational Enterprises* but legislative changes have also played a role. Thus ethical codes covering bribery and corruption are also seen as a way to enforce national legislation which in some cases implement the *OECD Anti-bribery Convention.*

Some national principles also specify what is regarded to be best practice in implementing corporate ethics. Thus the Commission on Public Trust and Private Enterprise in the United States calls for appropriate management processes to follow through on violations of the company's code of conduct. These should include programmes to ensure that employees understand, apply and adhere to the company's code of ethics and processes that encourage and make it safe for employees to raise non-compliance and other ethical issues. Prompt investigation of complaints and disciplinary action is also recommended in addition to intensive training programs.[71] Some "best practice" guidelines call for the compliance programme to come not under the ethics committee but to be an essential component of the internal audit process which usually reports to the audit committee of the board.[72]

Nomination of new board members

There is also a tendency to reinforce the effectiveness of the board (and in some cases to reduce the power of the CEO) by establishing a nomination committee, often with a recommendation that it also be staffed by independent directors. This is an area probably least developed by boards in executing their tasks. For example, although almost all the FTSE 100 companies have a nomination committee, for the remainder of the FTSE 350 the ratio is only 30 per cent. The Higgs Report also noted a high level of informality surrounding the process of appointing non-executive directors. Almost half of the non-executive directors surveyed for the report were recruited through personal contacts or friendships and only 4 per cent had had a formal interview. In Italy and Spain, a nominee's name and qualifications are not even included in proxy documents, a practice which has now led to complaints by some institutional investors. Less information is available for other countries although anecdotal evidence points to similar informality. However, some commentators have questioned the use of nomination committees on the grounds that this is a genuine shareholder function (see above). These concerns raise the issue of the mandate and duties of nomination committees and its composition. Elsewhere, there are a number of approaches to the issue. In Sweden some companies have created external committees composed of the larger shareholders, including the main institutional investors, and chaired by the chairman of the board. Such an external committee co-ordinates the selection/nomination process and lends transparency to the process. A similar situation exists in Norway. In Italy, a nomination committee is only required on a voluntary basis by the Preda code but compliance is minimal.[73]

The internal and external audit function

The manner in which audit tasks are organised varies greatly within the OECD. In a number of countries external auditors are appointed (at least formally) by the general meeting of shareholders – or in two tier systems by the supervisory board – and in others by the board itself. With respect to external audits, a number of recommendations move in the direction of ensuring that both the external and internal auditors are not intimidated by senior management or non-independent directors. Where there are audit committees of the board, a number of reports recommend that it comprise solely independent directors or a majority of independent directors.[74] Some, like the Blue Ribbon Report (1999), call for the committee to meet at least four times annually or more frequently as circumstances dictate. Generally speaking, recommendations and codes (including the set of principles established by IOSCO) call for an audit committee to be established as an important arm of the board and for it to form a nexus for the work of the internal auditor (Box 3.9).

The question of membership of audit committees has been given prominence by the Sarbanes-Oxley Act. However, the Act also raised for a while a number of difficult international issues. In the United States, audit committees must now be composed solely of independent directors with the sole authority to hire, supervise and fire the outside auditor. These requirements also extend to foreign private issuers of securities in the United States which at first implied that their corporate governance frameworks might need to be changed significantly. This has now been resolved to a great extent since the SEC has provided certain accommodation that takes into account foreign corporate governance schemes while ensuring that those with oversight responsibility for a company's outside auditors be independent of management. In Germany, employee representatives

Box 3.9. **Specifying the role of the audit committee: two examples**

As part of its *Principles of Auditor Independence and the Role of Corporate Governance in Monitoring an Auditor's Independence*, IOSCO has also established a set of broad principles covering auditor oversight:

- There should be a governance body that is in both appearance and fact independent of management of the entity being audited and acts in the interests of investors which should oversee the process of selection and appointment of the external auditor and the conduct of the audit.

- Such a committee or body (an "audit committee") within the entity's corporate structure should be the key representative body with which the external auditor interacts.

- The body should, on a regular and frequent basis, meet with the auditor without management present and discuss with the auditor any contentious issues that have arisen with management during the course of the audit and whether they have been satisfactorily resolved.

- The body should satisfy itself that the auditor is independent and should oversee the establishment of the entity's policies governing the performance of non-audit services by the auditor. It should also oversee policies regarding the employment by the entity of senior officers from the audit firm.

The committee should report to the shareholders on the actions it has taken to safeguard the independence of the auditor, including satisfying itself that the auditor is independent in accordance with applicable standards.

Such broad principles, which have also been issued by the European Commission, are often reflected in more detailed principles at the national level. Often these have been developed in response to a demand for greater clarity and to deal with different concepts. For example, in the UK the Smith report develops and codifies the role of audit committees, building on what is regarded as current best practice in that country. The guidance is intended to strengthen the hand of audit committees without breaking the unitary board structure.

The key points, which are reflected in the UK's Combined Code and in the detailed guidance, are:

Composition of the audit committee

- Committee to include at least three members, all independent non-executive directors.

- At least one member to have significant, recent and relevant financial experience, and suitable training to be provided to all.

Box 3.9. **Specifying the role of the audit committee: two examples** *(cont.)*

Role of the audit committee

- To monitor the integrity of the financial statements of the company, reviewing significant financial reporting judgements.

- To review the company's internal financial control system and, unless expressly addressed by a separate risk committee or by the board itself, risk management systems.

- To monitor and review the effectiveness of the company's internal audit function.

- To make recommendations to the board in relation to the external auditor's appointment; in the event of the board's rejecting the recommendation, the committee and the board should explain their respective positions in the annual report.

- To monitor and review the external auditor's independence, objectivity and effectiveness, taking into consideration relevant UK professional and regulatory requirements.

- To develop and implement policy on the engagement of the external auditor to supply non-audit services, taking into account relevant ethical guidance regarding the provision of non-audit services by the external audit firm.

In addition, the UK's Code requires that the committee should be provided with sufficient resources, that its activities should be reported in a separate section of the directors' report (within the annual report) and that the chairman of the committee should be present to answer questions at the AGM.

on the supervisory board are often involved in making decisions on audits (but they are not management) and in Japan and Italy company audit committees or boards (*kansayaku*) comprise non-executive directors. However, the traditional system in Japan (*kansayaku*) has often involved members with close relations to the firm even though they were non-executive directors. The recent amendment to the company law now requires that at least half of the *Kansayaku* board should be outsiders from 2005 and the definition of an outsider has been strengthened. In both Japan and Italy, companies can now also choose to adopt a unitary board system which requires an audit committee with independent directors. The SEC has also agreed to recognise the appointment of auditors by shareholder meetings – as is common in many countries – as long as the recommendation to the AGM has been made by the audit committee (or body performing similar functions) comprising independent directors.

Notes

1. In the United States, it is reported that investors seeking to put forward their own candidates must normally generate and circulate their own proxy ballots at a cost of some $250 000 or more. Management often packs its nominees into a single omnibus resolution, complicating shareholder efforts to cast separate votes for each director. In this case, the current proxy rules allow shareholders to indicate any specific nominees for which they are withholding their vote, but they cannot actually vote no. Their only choices are to vote in favour or withhold support. It is also reported that, depending on company bylaws, even a majority of withheld votes will fail to oust a director.

2. This is the conclusion reached by two Delaware judges for the United States. W. Chandler and L. Strine, *The New Federalism of the American Corporate System: Preliminary Reflections of Two Residents of One Small State*, February 2002, SSRN.

3. Chandler and Strine *op. cit.*, page 66.

4. The SEC released a report in July 2003 in which its staff recommended that the proxy process be changed in two areas: improved disclosure and improved shareholder access to the director nomination process. The report recommended that the SEC publish proposed rules for public comment that would require companies to disclose in their proxy statements information about a company's director nomination process and procedures for allowing shareholders to communicate with the board. On August 6th, the SEC proposed rules that would require these additional disclosures. The July report also recommended that the SEC propose and solicit public comments on new proxy rules that would allow shareholders to place their director nominees in a company's proxy materials subject to certain conditions, such as objective evidence of potential deficiencies in the proxy process indicating that majority shareholder views may not otherwise be adequately taken into account. The SEC received a record number of responses.

5. E. Tedesco, *Shareholder rights to file items on the agenda of a general meeting: Comparative study of Western European countries*, Hermes Discussion Paper, October 2002.

6. L.A. Bebchuk, *The case for empowering shareholders*, March 2003, SSRN.

7. More importantly, in Australia and the UK, shareholders also have the right to change the articles of association or any board decision by a majority of 75 per cent of the votes cast at a meeting. Moreover, they can initiate major decisions such as termination of the company. In the United States (Delaware law) shareholders also vote on changes to the articles of association but voting can take place only on proposals brought by the board of directors and a similar situation applies to other major decisions. See Bebchuk, *op. cit.*

8. Formally speaking, the corporation refusing a proposal requests a no action letter from SEC staff confirming that they will not recommend that the SEC take action against the company for excluding the shareholder proposal.

9. The new regulations in place since August 2002 require companies to produce an annual directors remuneration report which must include: a forward-looking report on remuneration policy, including details of performance criteria; details of each directors remuneration, including policy on directors contracts and an explanation of any compensation payments made in the previous financial year; disclosure requirements relating to the remuneration committee and a graph showing company performance.

10. *Report of the High Level Group of Company Law Experts on a Modern Regulatory Framework for Company Law in Europe*, Brussels, 2002.

11. See Bebchuk *op. cit.* for evidence that the actual remuneration packages differ in important respects from those that could be expected from arms length bargaining which would align incentives of managers with the interests of the shareholders. The emphasis of the Blue Ribbon Commission, *op. cit.*, on remuneration questions also suggests that shareholder oversight has not been very effective to date.

12. For OECD work in this area of disclosure see *Behind the corporate veil: using corporate entities for illicit purposes*, 2000. A template has been developed which provides a practical tool for assessing current systems for obtaining information on beneficial ownership and control of corporate entities. See *Options for obtaining beneficial ownership and control information*, OECD, 2002.

13. The study concludes that outside directors who fail to meet their "vigilance duties" almost never face personal liability. Greater liability under corporate and securities law is likely not to make a great difference given the mediating effects of insurance, indemnification and settlement incentives. B. Black, B. Cheffins and M. Klausner, "The vigilance duties and liability of outside directors", *John M. Ohlin Program in Law and Economics Working Paper*, 250.

14. K. Hopt, "Modern company and capital market problems: Improving European Corporate Governance after Enron", *ECGI Working Paper*, 05/2002.

15. Hopt *op. cit.*, page 22.

16. In September 2003, IOSCO issued a statement of principles covering both analysts and rating agencies: IOSCO Statement of Principles Regarding the Activities of Credit Rating Agencies and IOSCO Statement of Principles for Addressing Sell-side Securities Analyst Conflicts of Interest.

17. OECD *Economic Survey of Japan*, 2002.

18. Among the specific problems noted were voting by a show of hands in the UK, share-blocking in Italy, the concentration of meetings in Japan, and the hard copy delivery of proxy materials to registrars. See *Cross border proxy voting*, A report commissioned by the International Corporate Governance Network, 2003. Other institutions have identified share-blocking, powers of attorney and the lack of timely agenda documents as barriers. See for example, *www.hermes.co.uk/corporate-governance/intro.htm*.

19. *Mieux governer l'enterprise*, March 2003, *www.institutmontaigne.org*.

20. M. Hashimoto, "The pension fund association's recently released proxy voting principles", *Capital Research Journal*, Vol. 6, 2, 2003.

21. One study concludes that shares held by the bank in itself may lead to similar control outcomes in the US as pyramiding and cross shareholdings in other countries (*i.e.* after a point, performance declines). R. Adams and J. Santos, "Votes without dividends: Managerial control through bank trust departments", mimeo, *Federal Reserve Bank of New York*, March 2002.

22. T. Woidtke, *op. cit.* The author uses methods which address the potential for spurious results by taking account of the fact that the positive relation between shareholding in a firm and its performance might also run in the other direction.

23. A study by Romano appears to argue that shareholder activism has accomplished little, with no effect on the targeted firms' performance. However, the study really concerns one form of activism by public and union pension funds which may have

been motivated by other agendas than improving performance. In this sense the paper is compatible with Woidtke *op cit* findings. As most of the proposals were not accepted it is also hard to see how performance should have changed. R. Romano, "Less is more: Making shareholder activism a valuable mechanism of corporate governance", *Yale International Center for Finance Working Paper*, 00-10.

24. For a discussion of the different coalitions which may form between managers and the different stakeholders see M. Pagano and P. Volpin, "Managers, workers and corporate control", *ECGI Finance Working Paper*, 01/2002. For example, if private benefits of control are high and management owns a small equity stake, managers and employees might be natural allies vis-à-vis shareholders and the contestability of control. Employees may also act as white knights for the incumbent management.

25. For an explanation of the UK bidding system see G. Ferrarini, "Share ownership, takeover law and the contestability of corporate law", *Company Law reform in OECD countries: A comparative outlook of current trends*, Available at *www.oecd.org/daf/ corporate-governance*.

26. In most cases, the depository (Administration Office, *Stichting Administratiekantoor*) only grants proxies to exercise their voting rights to depository receipt holders up to 1 per cent of the company's share capital per person. These proxies are sometimes given only to natural persons. Under a new law before the parliament, the depository receipt holder can demand a proxy from the depository in order to vote. Whether there will be conditions to such a right was not known at the time of writing.

27. Johnson *et al., op. cit.*

28. One study examining actual control block transactions report control premia of over 30 per cent in Austria, Czech Republic, Italy, Mexico and Turkey. Belgium is not included in the study. See A. Dyke and L. Zingales, "Private benefits of control: an international comparison", *NBER Working Paper*, 8711, 2002. Other studies focus on differences in values among share classes.

29. For details of the reforms which will come into force at the beginning of 2004 see S. Cappiello and G. Marano, "The reform of the legal framework for Italian enterprises and the 2003 Company Law", *International Company and Commercial Law Review*, 6, 2003.

30. *Modernising Company Law and Enhancing Corporate Governance in the European Union – A Plan to Move Forward*, Commission of the European Communities, May 2003.

31. While holding out hope that progress is being made, one review stressed the problems in evaluating both the stated and actual commitment to stakeholder principles. See J. Cook and S. Deakin, "Stakeholding and corporate governance: theory and evidence on economic performance", in *Background Papers Prepared for the Corporate Law Review*, DTI, London, 2000.

32. In discussing barriers to exit and entry which affect the diffusion of new technologies, an OECD study (see *The New Economy: Beyond the Hype, op. cit.*, OECD, 2001) emphasised the role of personal bankruptcy. In a number of European countries creditors have claims on a bankrupt's assets for 6-10 years preventing entrepreneurs from starting again. They might also be forbidden from being a company director or from receiving bank finance. In Japan, apart from the social stigma tied to personal bankruptcy, which is also a factor in continental Europe, there is no protection of the bankrupt's home as there is in the US and in other countries. All this may limit incentives to undertake risky projects leading to less

innovation and slower growth. The study also noted that the lack of automatic protection from creditors in Japan and Korea provided few incentives for a company to declare bankruptcy, allowing crippled companies to continue their operations. In the meantime, there have been significant changes to the law in Korea to deal with this issue. In Japan, the under-development of debtor in possession financing is a problem as well as the fact that companies only tend to file once they are insolvent. The new Civil Rehabilitation Law has now lowered the threshold for creditor agreement from two thirds to a half and can also protect vital assets from creditors. It is now an increasingly used method for dealing with debt problems. See *OECD Economic Survey of Japan*, 2002.

33. For example see S. Claessens and L. Klapper, *Bankruptcy around the world*, mimeo, 2002.

34. A key study using an aggregate indicator of creditor rights is R. LaPorta *et al.*, "Law and finance", *Journal of Political Economy*, 106, 1998. Their indicator comprised five variables but work by Claessens and Klapper *op. cit.* indicates that there is substitution between the elements suggesting that simple aggregation is not appropriate. More importantly, R. Broggi and P. Santella, *Two new measures of bankruptcy efficiency*, mimeo, 2003, take a more general approach for five countries looking at a wider number of characteristics. This changes country rankings quite substantially in comparison with the La Porta rankings. In particular, the regime in Sweden appears to be much more efficient than is often considered to be the case.

35. For example, a supplier putting in place plant to service only one client will usually have contracts with the purchaser which covers the risk of loss and financing arrangements for the project will normally reflect this issue. See O.E. Williamson, "Corporate finance and corporate governance", *Journal of Finance*, 1988 and also O.E. Williamson, "The theory of the firm as governance structure: from choice to contract", *Journal of Economic Perspectives*, 16, 2002.

36. In particular, it is important that the productivity estimates controls for industry effects as when high tech industries have high productivity and grant ESOPS. However, what is found is a level rather than a growth rate effect so that this possible problem might be less than would be the case if the effect centred on growth rates.

37. For the general approach see E. Schlicht, "Social evolution, corporate culture and exploitation", *IZA Bonn Discussion Paper*, 651, 2002 and for preliminary empirical work see J. Deckop *et al.*, "Getting more than you pay for: organisational citizenship behaviour and pay for performance plans", *Academy of Management Journal* , 42, 1999.

38. There is by now a rich but not unproblematic literature about the effects of works councils in Germany. Part of the methodological problem is to separate the decision to have a works council from the subsequent effects. Moreover, it appears to be necessary to also consider the qualitative nature of the works council. Not surprisingly, results are quite contradictory although the effect on the level of productivity appears to be positive. For a review see B. Frick and E. Lehmann, *Corporate governance in Germany: Ownership, codetermination and firm performance in a stakeholder economy*, mimeo, 2002.

39. This is the thrust of J. Tirole, "Corporate governance", *Econometrica*, 69, 2001.

40. A number of studies use *Fortune's* reputational survey but such indices are related to prior financial performance and suffer from the "halo effect". For a review which concludes with a not proven health warning see J. Cook and S. Deakin, *op. cit.*

41. For instance, it is agued in Europe that quarterly reports could lead to excessive emphasis on the short run. This might be so but when the debate refers to the US experience to support its case that is one step too far. In the US it was the peculiar options schemes paid to a number of executives – and not quarterly reporting *per se* – and the possibility for large stock price swings which created powerful incentives for some executives to attempt to drive up prices with optimistic quarterly reporting.

42. Shroder Saloman Smith Barney "UK defined benefit pensions: the trustees' nightmare", October 2002.

43. In several countries (*e.g.* the US) there are requirements for the auditor to evaluate the relationship of a specialist (*i.e.* the actuary) to the client including circumstances that might impair the specialist's objectivity. How effective such provisions have been remains an open question, especially in view of calls for tightening audit standards around the world.

44. For example see the various contributions in the *Report of the Group of Thirty, op. cit.*

45. Canada also has a well developed regulatory impact methodology. For the UK example see *Regulatory Impact Assessment: Operating and financial review, www.dti.gov.uk/companiesbill/financialreview.pdf.*

46. In May 2003 the European Commission proposed to the European Parliament a modernisation of the 8th Directive to provide a comprehensive legal basis for statutory audits conducted within the EU.

47. The relevant documents are: *Principles of Auditor Independence and the Role of Corporate Governance in Monitoring an Auditor's Independence,* and *Principles of Auditor Oversight.* Both were released in October 2002.

48. In its discussion paper the committee recognised "the tension between setting any minimum reporting requirements high enough to allow reasonable comparison between organisations, including use of the same metrics, and avoiding an over-prescriptive approach that might stifle innovation, prejudice commercial confidentiality or be unduly burdensome". *Accounting for People,* Task Force on Human Capital Management, London, May 2003. *www.accountingforpeople.gov.uk.*

49. New regulatory requirements in the UK, France, Germany and Australia require investors (usually only pension funds) to disclose their investment policies on environmental, social and ethical issues.

50. These include the Global Reporting Initiative. *www.globalreporting.org/.*

51. See *Business Approaches to Combating Bribery,* Background study prepared for the OECD Corporate Responsibility roundtable, June 2003. *www.oecd.org/dataoecd/63/57/2638716.pdf.*

52. For an example of verification guidelines see *www.globalreporting.org/* and *www.accountability.org.uk.*

53. For a strong defence of the role of insiders see S. Bainbridge, "A critique of the NYSE's director independence listing standards", *Securities Regulation Law Journal,* Vol. 30, 2002.

54. One can accept the presence of serious weaknesses without going as far as P. Davies who concluded that "… the German supervisory board continues to be a rather ineffective monitor, whereas the UK board has not only taken on the monitoring task formally but is better placed to discharge it effectively in practice". P. Davies,

"Board structure in the UK and Germany: Convergence or continuing divergence?", *International and Comparative Law Journal*, 2, 2000.

55. As K. Hopt observes, mandatory labour co-determination does not fit well with such a choice. Legislators will have to find a formula for how to have labour co-determination in the one tier board of the future German *societas europaea* without frightening off foreign companies interested in creating such a European entity together with a German partner. K. Hopt, "Modern company and capital market problems improving European corporate governance after Enron", *ECGI Law working Paper*, 5, 2002.

56. The *kansayaku* auditors are observers in board meetings and their role was redefined in 1974 to include monitoring and policing of management decisions. The corporate law revision in 1993 further specified that for large corporations the *kansayaku* board should comprise three people with a minimum of one from outside the firm. By 2005 the number of outsiders is to be raised to at least one half. The *Kansayaku* are charged with overseeing directors including the chairman of the board who have usually been promoted internally.

57. The SEC recently adopted a safe harbour so that a person who is not an executive officer or shareholder owning 10 per cent or more of any class of voting equity securities will not be deemed independent for the purposes of serving on the audit committee. The SEC's adopting release does, however, note that 10 per cent is not the upper limit to prove independent status (*i.e.* non-affiliate status). Nevertheless, Chandler and Strine *op. cit.* fear that such limits will establish more than a safe harbour and lead enforcement away from the current practice in the US of looking at the specific transaction and the situation surrounding it in judging whether a director was capable of acting independently.

58. Research commissioned for the Higgs Report also showed that while there might be a tension, there was no essential contradiction between monitoring and strategic aspects of the role of non-executive director.

59. The report does indeed take this view and argues that the recruitment process by companies needs to be improved. To stimulate such an improvement it recommends initiatives by civil society groups to monitor and analyse developments. It also calls for better training of board members. See *The Tyson Report on the Recruitment and Development of Non-executive Directors*, London Business School, 2003.

60. It is also worth noting that at Enron, Worldcom and Globalcrossing, the positions were split, although the Chairman was not independent.

61. However, in his far ranging report on MCI/WorldCom, Breedon has proposed such a separation for a major US company. See R. Breedon, *Restoring Trust*, New York, August 2003.

62. Thus the dissenting voice on the Commission (actually from a large pension fund) stated that "good corporate governance has never created a great company – great leaders, great CEOs have done so". The context is one of good corporate governance as a necessary though not sufficient condition.

63. Such questions are discussed in the consultative document, "*Rewards for failure*"; *Directors remuneration, contracts, performance and severance*, Consultative Document, Department of Trade and Industry, London, 2003, *www.dti.gov.uk/cld/published.htm*, and entry on directors remuneration.

64. See L. Bebchuk, J. Fried and D. Walker *op. cit.*

65. The New York Times, 18 December 2002.

66. J. Core, R. Holthausen and D. Larcker, "Corporate governance, Chief executive compensation and firm performance", *Journal of Financial Economics*, 51, 1999. See also references to other work in Bebchuk *et al.*

67. For example see *Executive Compensation*, Report to the Investment Committee, 16 June 2003, CALPERS and *Executive Remuneration*, A Report to the International Corporate Governance Network, July 2002.

68. U. Bhattacharya and H. Daouk, "The world price of insider trading", *Journal of Finance*, forthcoming. The authors found that the cost of equity in a country does not change after the introduction of insider trading laws but decreases significantly after the first prosecution. It would be informative to know whether the intensity of enforcement has a similar effect.

69. *OECD Guidelines for Multinational Enterprises*, *www.oecd.org/daf/investment/guidelines*.

70. For one review see H. Gregory and J. Pollack, "Corporate social responsibility", *Global Counsel*, March 2002.

71. Enforcement of ethical conduct was also a key issue raised in the MCI/WorldCom report by R. Breedon, *op. cit.*

72. See for example, The Conference Board, *Corporate Governance Best Practices*, New York, 2003.

73. Only 14 companies out of a sample of 104 listed companies (comprising 68 per cent of listed companies) had a nomination committee but even here some used it only for board appointments to subsidiaries. However, 10 per cent of all listed companies have a cumulative voting system so that minority shareholders are able to elect at least one member of the board. See *Analisi dello stato di attuazione del Codice di Autodisciplina delle societa quotate*, Assonime, Rome February 2003.

74. In Italy there is a separate board of auditors elected by the AGM. The minority must be represented on this board.

CORPORATE GOVERNANCE: A SURVEY OF OECD COUNTRIES – ISBN 92-64-10605-7 – © OECD 2004

OECD PUBLICATIONS, 2, rue André-Pascal, 75775 PARIS CEDEX 16
PRINTED IN FRANCE
(26 2004 01 1 P) ISBN 92-64-10605-7 – No. 53391 2004